The

Marlborough Branch

FOR

Chris Watts - in memory of his Grandfather

Note on track plans

To show the comparitive sizes of each location all track plans have
been reproduced at the uniform scale of approximately two chains to
one inch.

Published by
IRWELL PRESS
3 Durley Avenue, Pinner, Middlesex, HA5 1JQ
Printed by The Amadeus Press Ltd
Huddersfield, West Yorkshire

The
Marlborough Branch

The Railways of Savernake and Marlborough

by

Kevin Robertson & David Abbott

IRWELL
PRESS

SKETCH MAP
SWINDON AND CHELTENHAM EXTENSION RAILWAY.

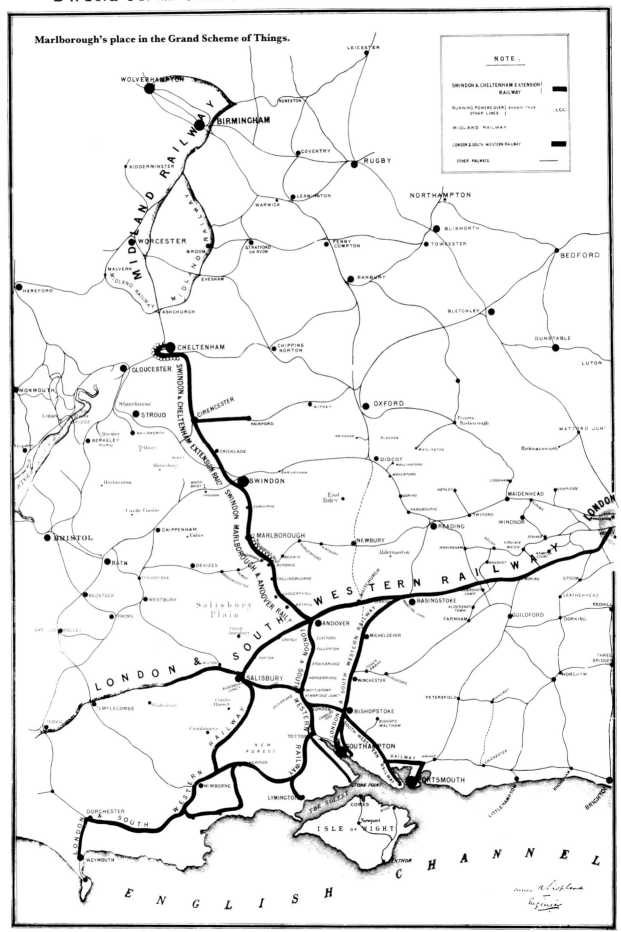

Marlborough's place in the Grand Scheme of Things.

Contents

ACKNOWLEDGEMENTS

Without the assistance of a number of individuals the compilation of this book would not have been possible and we would like then to record our grateful thanks to the following;
Mike Barnsley, David Bartholomew, Neville Bridger, British Rail, David Chandler, David Hyde, Gordon King, Jeremy Page, The Public Record Office at Kew, Marlborough College and in particular D.R.C. West Esq., Roger Pope, Roger Simmonds, the Historical Model Railway Society, Paul Karau, the National Railway Museum, the late Tom Sands, the Signalling Record Society, Paul Strong, the Swindon Society and in particular Brian Bridgeman, Adrian Vaughan, Chris Watts, The Wiltshire Record Office at Trowbridge and Graham Wirdman. And of course to George and Chris for their advice and encouragement.
We would also like to thank our respective wives, Margaret and Lyn. Especially for the typing, telephone answering, and even more important coffee and biscuits. A message for Margaret - *now you can have the dining room table back.*

A superb view of Savernake station, looking west prior to the doubling of the main line. It can be dated as sometime between 1883 and 1893, as after this date a rapid change was made to signals, showing red and green lights at night time. The one in view, besides being of the slotted type, is fitted with just a single spectacle plate which showed either a red or a white light to the engine driver. In the background can be seen the open footbridge and road overbridge whilst in the distance it is possible to make out the new Savernake West signal box, in the 'V' of the junction formed by the divergence of the Marlborough branch. The Metro tank is standing in the solitary siding then existing on the up side, which is seen to possess a loading gauge - this was removed at an unknown date. On the extreme left is the end of the down loop, later cut back in consequence of the extension of the platform. At the time the photograph was taken the station was served by trains on the Berks and Hants Extension line as well as local services to Marlborough and SMA (MSWJ) trains, the through service between Swindon and Andover having commenced on 5th February 1883. It is believed the cost of the station as first built amounted to £1,690.

INTRODUCTION

Contemplating this book, it was with some trepidation that we set out to chronicle the history of The Marlborough Railway, a line which closed to passenger traffic almost fifty years ago. Just over five miles long with a single line of rails it possessed no intermediate stations, passing loops or major civil engineering features. In brief a line which appeared at first glance to offer little scope for study and foolishly perhaps, we thought one could be written in the space of a few short pages.

The fortunes of its near neighbour, the Midland and South Western Junction railway have been chronicled in depth, and in consequence the little Marlborough Branch has for long lived in its shadow. How wrong then could our first assumptions have been, for in the course of study a wealth of material has been uncovered, whilst it even proved possible to trace the relatives of former members of staff from all those years ago. Even so we would be the first to admit that many questions lie unanswered and will now in all probability remain that way.... Oh for a time warp!

The intention at the outset had been to confine our writings to the Marlborough Railway and to leave all but the barest reference to its neighbour, the Swindon, Marlborough and Andover. (which later became the Midland and South Western Junction - so the confusion begins!) This though was quickly found not only to be impossible but also impractical, for the fortunes of the two lines were shared for many years and as a result one is privileged to delve into the rivalry and even at times hostility which existed between the various parties.

Competition had led to two separate and independent railways in the Marlborough/Savernake area, a situation which existed for some 35 years. For a short time there was also a railway operated bus service competing for the same traffic, providing for a 'battle royal,' not always obvious to the travelling public.

History would later - so often the case - totally reverse this order of events; the first seeds of change came into effect soon after, when the GWR took over the MSWJR route in 1923. Paddington then chose to shut the former Marlborough Railway route and instead concentrate all traffic on the tracks of its former arch enemy. This method of economy - or perhaps the word is rationalisation, must have been almost unique in those days, although from a practical view point it was sensible and in many respects an obvious way of integration, thirty years before Dr. Beeching was to carry out similar work elsewhere.

The story then of the Marlborough Railway has all the ingredients of a melodrama in which there were many outspoken players. The great and good certainly had their say, in the person of Felix Pole, later perhaps the greatest General Manager the GWR ever possessed.

Composing this narrative some fifty five years after the branch closed, it is sad to reflect on how little survives today; a bridge abutment or overgrown earthworks the only clues to what was once a thriving railway and commercial lifeline. Marlborough and Savernake are now devoid of railway communication, with some unaware it had ever been otherwise.

But this is not intended to be a book of mere sentiment, for trains still pass the site of the station at Savernake even if the speeding passenger in his air-conditioned carriage has but to blink to miss it. For no longer does the branch engine whistle before leaving for Marlborough.

David Abbott
Kevin Robertson
1990

49194   MARLBOROUGH   VALENTINES SERIES

The station, as it could be observed from the southern slopes of Postern Hill in 1908, with 'Cherry Orchard' leading up towards the railway. The large white structure between the engine shed and main buildings was a road motor garage which was probably new in 1904, to coincide with the commencement of the bus service to Calne. The high level - no pun intended - of the station compared with the church tower is apparent with the railway on what was then (and indeed still is) the southern fringes of the town.

1

Marlborough High Street looking east, the Town Hall in the centre background and St. Mary's church behind. The width of the roadway through the High Street is said to be equal to that of a Saxon *lynchet*.

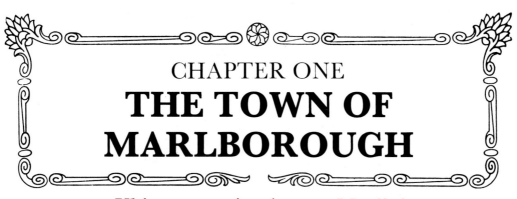

CHAPTER ONE
THE TOWN OF MARLBOROUGH

Ubi nunc sapientis ossa Merlini
- Where now are the bones of wise Merlin?

The county of Wiltshire is arguably foremost in beauty amongst the southern shires of England, an area bounded to the north by the county of Gloucester and the Cotswold Hills. To the south a similar if lesser range extends from west to east, a chalk ridge laid down many millions of years past, made famous by the horse carvings hewn from the chalk at its varying high points and visible from miles around.

For centuries Wiltshire existed as a prime agricultural area with Salisbury, Devizes and Bath its main sources of commerce. Prior to the coming of the railways, Marlborough was the only other location of any importance. Agriculture was the main occupation for the inhabitants of numerous villages; the fertile earth is ideal for the raising of both crops and livestock and the numbers of cattle easily outnumber the human population.

According to J.E.Chandler, renowned local historian, Marlborough may be described as the *Gateway to Ancient Britain*, a justifiable claim (though such matters are subject to constant revision) on the basis that ten thousand years ago early man selected the area of the present town as the first known settlement in the country.

Over the ensuing millennia countless changes have been wrought upon the district, changes so aptly described in the nineteenth century by F.E.Hulme, who when speaking of Marlborough referred to it thus:

We live in the burial mounds of nameless warriors. We see even the history of our small town is woven into the national life, and, following its history in no petty provincial spirit, we learn how stirring is our island story. The men of countless generations sleep around us in the dust, and all the past speaks to us in warning or encouragement. Be it ours to hand the torch on, that shall brightly illuminate the coming days, and prove ourselves no unworthy descendants of the men who, in the forefront of battle, gave their lives for England, and died that liberty might live.

Although granted its first charter by King John in 1204* there is much of interest prior to this date. Indeed in name alone there have been many variations of the present spelling of Marlborough, including:

Maer-lea-beorg - Circa 522, and thought to refer to the Mound by the Boundary Pasture.
Maerlebi in 1072 - this reference from the reign of William I. is taken from the spelling which appears on a silver penny minted in the town.
Marleberge, 1091
aet Marle beorg, 1150
Mallesberiense Castellum, 1140
Merleberga, 1148
Melleberga,1175
de Merleborowe, 1361
Marleburg, 1428
Marborowe, 1485

The influence of the French and more particularly Normandy is self evident from the spellings, whilst the common denominator of 'berg - borowe' etc may be taken to refer to the Mound. This is reputed to be the oldest construction in the town and is now within the confines of Marlborough College. Certainly by the time a Charter was granted the legend had arisen that this was the burial place of Merlin, although interestingly no archaeological excavations have ever been carried out. Of Merlin himself, little in the way of facts are known except that he was supposed to originate from Ireland, his remaining life interwoven over the centuries to become legend. But as a theory could his name have been given over to the town adjacent to his supposed last resting place? Indeed this connotation would perhaps seem the most obvious, 'Merlberow - the burial place of Merlin. Surprisingly such an obvious choice seems to have been overlooked in the past and instead the connection is with *marl* the major composite soil of the area. Another suggestion is that Marl may have been the name given to an early British chieftain or warrior. A comparable theory is applied to the naming of Silbury Hill, which dates from a similar period.

Besides the references above a number of other spellings are to be found in old documents and plans including; *Marelberg(e)*, *Malbrow*, *Marleborrow*, *Marleburgh*, *Merleberg(e)*, *Mierleb*, *Merligesboroe*, *Marlebourough*, *Mierlrow*, *Moulbrough*, *Marleboro*, *Marleborowe*, *Marleboarough*, *Marlebourough*, *Morlebrought*, *Marlebury*, *Merlbury*, *Marlburg*, *Mearleah*, *Marlesbeorg* and perhaps the strangest of them all, *Mrlbrei*. The present spelling of Marlborough was in use certainly a few years after the granting of the first Charter in 1204. It appears then to have lapsed into disuse, superseded by some of the other references to reappear a number of centuries later.

Long before its first Charter, Marlborough - the present spelling will be used from hereon - was an isolated place. The settlements of the area were by necessity self contained. Indeed what is now the lush greenery of the present Kennet valley to the east was little more than a tangle of forest and swamp. The river itself was probably far larger than that recognised today, although there is no record of its use in connection with access to the settlement. The line of forest extended west and north to Savernake, the village of Marlborough lying not far above the river level. This is somewhat strange as an essential prerequisite in those days was command of a good view over the surrounding lands.

* Besides the Charter of King John in 1204, similar statements were provided for at a number of other dates, by Henry III in 1229 and again in 1246, by Henry IV in 1408, Henry V in 1414, Elizabeth I in 1576, by Oliver Cromwell in 1657 and in 1688 by James II.

With the coming of the Romans and their roads for military use the first semblance of access to and from the town can be traced. East to west was the London to Bath road whilst north to south came the road from Cirencester to Salisbury and Winchester, the latter forking into two prior to entering Savernake forest. There is evidence of a Roman settlement at the top of what is now the London Road Hill on the A4. Later came a move to a new camp called *Cunetio* in the water meadows close to the Mildenhall road although at the time referred to as *the Black Field*. This was the nearest site to Marlborough thought to have been used by the Romans although it possibly remained in use for some time by 'Romanised Britains' after the legions finally departed in 410 A.D.

As elsewhere the period from 410 A.D. for almost six centuries is drowned in obscurity. It is for this reason that it is referred to as the 'Dark Ages'. What is known is that during this period of Saxon occupation a settlement grew up around the area of the green mound, probably chosen as it was less prone to flooding compared with *Cunetio*. The mound was fortified with a moat and stockade. From this it may be assumed that the settlement was anticipating invasion or battle, and indeed it is known that threats were issued against the area of Wessex, of which Marlborough was a part, from the ever growing armies of Mercia. Battles are known to have been fought at several sites nearby but the enemies were not always from Mercia; the strife was tribal between the Saxons and Britons and shaped much of the area. Victory for the Saxon invaders gave them full control of what is now the county of Wiltshire.

The Saxons brought with them new and improved methods of farming, in particular the establishment of 'lynchets,' or as they may perhaps be more easily described hillside terraces.

Several examples of these earthworks remain to this day on the side of Granham Hill and can be seen from the Pewsey Road, although care should be taken not to confuse them with the numerous bridle ways and pony treks criss - crossing the same area. It is also worth mentioning that the original width of such lynchets is said to equal the width of the present High Street, and traces of them can be found at the rear of some houses.

Up to the time of the Norman Conquest, the Saxons divided the country into areas known as Hundreds. Marlborough being in the Hundred of Selkley, similar in name to the small village of Selsey on the Sussex coast, though whether this was the actual historic connection is unknown. Following the succession of William I, the history of Marlborough becomes clearer. The settlement around the Mound became a castle though fortified only with timber. Stone was used later, probably from 1175 onwards. The influence of King William had been felt in the town very soon for by 1070 the Monarch had arranged for Agelric, Bishop of the South Saxons to be imprisoned in the town and although it is not mentioned whereabouts this occurred, it may be reasonable to assume the castle was used. A mint was also established with coins produced certainly up to the first years of the reign of William II. Shortly after this in 1195 is the first reference to the Town or Port Mill, itself an initial source of local dispute. The necessity for a head of water for the Mill caused flooding in the vicinity of Stonebridge Lane with the resultant wrath of the locals (the name Stonebridge is somewhat misleading here and should not be taken as the literal name). Sarsen stones bridged the river at this point which flooded, as mentioned, at regular intervals. To combat this, and the irate residents, a large stone known as the Culverstone was

COLLEGE GATES, MARLBOROUGH.   205556.

Part of the entrance to Marlborough College, which saw its first scholars in 1843. The college has had a number of famous old boys, including Sir John Betjeman, whilst other equally renowned names have emanated from the town, including Cardinal Wolsey.

Tottenham House **in Savernake Forest. The ancestral home of the Marquisate of Ailesbury, its family would play an important part in bringing the railway to Marlborough.**

placed upstream with the millers forbidden to allow the water to cover it. Accordingly ease of passage over the River Kennet was assured.

Besides William I a number of other Norman and Plantagenet Kings were regular visitors to Marlborough, including Henry III who held court over his parliament in the town in 1267. The great attraction was the hunting offered by Savernake Forest, although Henry VIII is known to have visited whilst travelling to Wulfhall(sic), to see Jane Seymour, reputed to be his favourite wife.

But we have jumped ahead somewhat and it is necessary to return to the time of Henry VII and the strength of the monarchy following the Wars of the Roses. Together with the coming of gunpowder this conflict spelt the end of the castle; no longer were its towers impregnable and their demise was imminent; few traces of it can be found today. Gradually the various communities surrounding the Mound merged and were eventually linked by the building of the High Street. The development of the town was of course slow but nevertheless various churches were erected and in 1550 the grammatical school was founded, later to become, in 1843, the college itself.

The Civil War visited itself upon the town and Marlborough, of strategic importance on the road to the west made for several battles, though they were small in comparison to those fought at Wash Common and Donnington Castle near Newbury. There was sufficient opposition between King and Cromwell to leave pistol ball marks on many of the buildings and churches. The Civil War over, the town suffered a more damaging blow than any of the warring factions had thrown at it over the years. Starting in a tanner's house at the west end of High Street a fire, 'the like ...never seen in England before', all

Aside from its status as Royal Forest, Savernake has for many years been in the charge of the Forestry Commission, which has regulated the growth and felling of timber. In times of conflict in particular, much of it was sent out from Savernake, for a variety of uses. Horses hauled the loads well into the present century.

The Kennet and Avon Canal at Savernake, at the east end of the Bruce Tunnel. Barges were moved by horse, though for the distance of the tunnel the bargee would haul his vessel along by hand, using a chain fixed to the tunnel wall, the horse being walked over the top of the tunnel via a pathway. In this view the barge *Unity*, loaded with timber, is heading west towards Burbage whilst the horse waits to be led to the other end of the tunnel. Above the tunnel mouth can be seen the GWR Berks & Hants Extension Railway, with Savernake East signal box.

but destroyed the town in 1653. Two less disastrous conflagrations took place in 1679 and 1690. A number of buildings making up the High Street today, however, still boast a most interesting past, including the present day Merlin Restaurant, reputedly the site of Henry III's Parliament of 1267.

An aspect of Marlborough history, now almost forgotten, is the extraordinary autonomy the Mayor enjoyed with local Borough matters. Quarter Sessions were also held in the town and punishments varied from the gallows to the stocks, pillory and ducking stool. Borough records show that the actual stool was made in 1578 at a price of 7/6d (37½p)

The various Charters over the years allowed fairs and markets to be held in Marlborough, notably a weekly meeting on the Green on Wednesdays and Saturdays. The same site was used for the annual sheep fair until it ceased in 1893. A later change of location ensured the markets were held in the High Street where they continue to the present day. Horse racing brought many visitors to the town between 1840 and 1887 when a meet was held on the Common. Previously this had been at the nearby Barton Down.

The Castle Inn boasts a complex history which would need a single volume to cover its past. However, suffice to say that it had a long association with the Seymour family and Henry VIII. It was quickly established as the finest Inn on the road from London to Bath with as many as 40 coaches a week calling there at its peak in the late 18th and early 19th century. Despite such lavish provision it is important not to lose sight of the fact that the roads of the period were really little better than modern day farm tracks, ruts and potholes abounding and in winter hampered by seemingly endless torrents of mud. Regardless of these difficulties the stage coach provided a link with the outside world. The journey from Bristol to London occupied three days with a stopover in Marlborough, which of course explains the number of beds (60) available at the *Castle*. The fortunes of the stage coach operators and the inn keepers were, however, to be short lived for already there were stirrings towards a new mode of transport, the canals. With the opening of the Kennet and Avon Canal navigation throughout in 1810, the first seeds were sown in what was to be a complete revolution in transport for the borough.

THE
PUBLIC CONVEYANCES
FROM THE
YORK HOUSE, BATH
Royal Mail Office,
Are constructed upon the most approved principles of safety.

SHOULD ANY
IRREGULARITIES OCCUR
IT IS REQUESTED THAT
Immediate Application
BE MADE TO
WILLIAM LANE.

ROYAL MAIL AND GENERAL COACH OFFICE,
YORK HOUSE, BATH.

Royal Mails.

LONDON—through Devizes, Marlborough, and Reading, every Evening at a quarter past Seven.

LONDON—through Chippenham and Calne, every Evening at Eight.

EXETER—through Wells, Bridgewater, and Taunton, every Morning at Seven.

PLYMOUTH and DEVONPORT direct—through Totness, every Morning at Seven, and arrives the same Evening at half-past Nine.

FALMOUTH—through Truro and Launceston, every Morning at Seven.

BARNSTAPLE and ILFRACOMBE through Wiveliscombe and South Molton, every Morning at a-quarter before Seven.

PORTSMOUTH (*New Mail*)—through Warminster, Salisbury, and Southampton, every Evening at a quarter past Eight.

CHELTENHAM — through Tetbury and Cirencester, every Afternoon at half-past Two.

BIRMINGHAM MANCHESTER, through Gloucester and Worcester, every Afternoon at half-past Four.

MILFORD, HAVERFORDWEST, through Swansea and Carmarthen, every Morning at Six.

BRISTOL and CLIFTON—every Morning at Five and Six, and Afternoon at Three and half-past Four.

Post Coaches.

LONDON, (*York House Day Coach*), in 11 hours, through Chippenham, Marlborough, and Reading, every Morning at Seven, to the Gloucester Coffee House, Piccadilly, and Belle Sauvage, Ludgate Hill.

LONDON, (*Regulator*), in 11 hours, same route, every Morning at half-past Eight, to the Hatchett's Hotel, Piccadilly, and Bull and Mouth, St. Martin's le Grand.

LONDON, (*Emerald*), in 11 hours, through Devizes, every Morning at half-past Eight, to the Gloucester Coffee House, Piccadilly, and Spread Eagle, Gracechurch-street. No Fees.

LONDON, (*Monarch*), through Chippenham and Calne, every Evening, at Seven, to the Hatchett's Hotel, Piccadilly, and Belle Sauvage, Ludgate Hill. No Fees.

READING, (*Star*), through Devizes, Marlborough, and Newbury, every Morning (except Sunday), at Ten.

EXETER, (*Retaliator*), through Wells, Glastonbury, Somerton, Langport, Ilminster, and Honiton, every Morning (except Sunday), at half-past Eight.

SIDMOUTH, every Morning at a-quarter past Eight.

LYME, through Shepton Mallet, Ilchester, and Axminster, Monday, Wednesday, and Friday Mornings, at Eight.

PLYMOUTH AND DEVONPORT, through Chudleigh, every Morning, (Sunday excepted) at half past 8.

SOUTHAMPTON, (*Rocket*), through Warminster, Salisbury, and Romsey, Monday, Wednesday and Friday Mornings, at Eight.

BIRMINGHAM, (*York House Coach*), through Stroud, Painswick, and Tewkesbury, every Morning, (except Sunday), at Eight.

CHELTENHAM, WORCESTER, and SHREWSBURY, every Morning, (except Sunday), at a quarter before Eight.

BRIGHTON, (*Red Rover*), in 13 hours, through Warminster, Salisbury, Southampton, Chichester, Arundell, and Worthing, Tuesday, Thursday, and Saturday Mornings, at Eight.

The Red Rover is the only Coach that arrives at Southampton in time for the Steam Packets to Cowes, Ryde, &c.

PORTSMOUTH AND GOSPORT, every Morning (except Sunday), at Eight.

WARWICK, LEAMINGTON, AND COVENTRY, every Morning (except Sunday), at Eight.

LIVERPOOL, every Morning (Sunday excepted), at a quarter before Eight, and Afternoon at half-past Four.

WEYMOUTH, (*Wellington*) through Frome, Bruton, Sherborne, and Dorchester, Monday, Wednesday, and Friday Mornings, at half-past Eight.

This Coach arrives in time for the Government Steam Packet to Jersey, Guernsey, &c.

OXFORD, (*Oxonian*) through Chippenham, Swindon, and Farringdon, every Monday, Wednesday, and Friday Mornings, at half-past Eight.

MANCHESTER, CARLISLE, and EDINBURGH, every Morning, (except Sunday), at a quarter before Eight.

CHESTER AND HOLYHEAD, every Morning, (except Sunday), at Eight, and Afternoon at half-past Two.

OXFORD, (*Collegian*) through Tetbury & Cirencester, every Morning (Sunday excepted), at Nine.

DEVIZES, every Afternoon, (except Sunday), at a quarter past Five.

WESTON - SUPER - MARE AND CLEVEDON, (*Sovereign*) every Morning at half-past Seven.

CLIFTON, every Morning at a quarter before Ten, and Afternoon at Three.

BRISTOL, Coaches every hour.

Every Information may be obtained at this Office relative to the Steam Packets to Ireland, South Wales, &c.

WILLIAM LANE, Proprietor.

Part of the *Grand Avenue* through Savernake Forest and the original access to Tottenham House, home of the Marquess of Ailesbury. This driveway runs through the Forest for nearly five miles and is bounded by beech, ash, oak and chestnut as well as a number of more recently planted and fast growing species. The natural obstacle of the Forest precluded the Berks and Hants Extension Railway passing through Marlborough.

CHAPTER TWO
EARLY RAILWAY SCHEMES

The natural obstacle of the chalk downs near Marlborough precluded a place for the town on the original Great Western line between London and Bristol. Brunel determined upon a route running north of the hills through the village of Swindon, later to develop into a thriving town. The 'main line', as it afterwards became known opened fully (London - Bristol) to traffic on 30th June 1841.

Shortly after this came the period referred to as 'Railway Mania', which saw a number of schemes proposed for lines running basically north - south, and serving Marlborough. But the promoters of these schemes saw their main benefit as a direct connection with the Midlands and the south coast. Any additional traffic in between was regarded as a bonus, for as already mentioned, Marlborough itself was but a small prize, and by comparison unlikely to generate much extra trade.

These proposals were varied and numerous, the first and probably most ambitious being a scheme to connect Manchester and Southampton. A line would run from the Midland Railway at Cheltenham through Cirencester, Marlborough and Andover; 'The South and Midlands Junction Railway', from Bicester to Swindon and Salisbury was also proposed, with branches to both Marlborough and Devizes, whilst another scheme envisaged a 'Manchester, Southampton and Poole Railway,' running south of the downs near Savernake. For a variety of reasons the schemes were to founder; the optimism of the promoters insufficient to overcome the strength of opposition - often from the Great Western, who feared that their monopoly of traffic would be jeopardised and the situation thus emerged of the Great Western in the role of the ogre, to these entrepreneurial ventures. It is an aspect of the GWR which authors in the past have tended to play down and yet clearly demonstrates a finely honed business acumen, as well as a ruthless will to strangle and gobble up all opposition. Growth was achieved by seemingly small concessions, an agreement for running powers or laying of narrow gauge track alongside its broad gauge routes. To the GWR directors this was far preferable to a direct competitor for the same traffic.

It was then, some years before new lines of railway began to encroach into Wiltshire. The nominally independent (Great Western backed), Berks and Hants line opened from Reading to Hungerford in 1847 and the Devizes branch from Holt ten years later. Shortly afterwards proposals were mooted for an extension of the Berks and Hants from Hungerford to connect at Devizes which, it was originally hoped, would run through Marlborough itself. It was now that the natural obstacle of the chalk downs played its part, for the route chosen was actually south of the town, nearer to Savernake and for some distance almost parallel to the Kennet and Avon Canal

The traders and men of influence from Marlborough were indignant at this; the railway had missed the town and the local worthies were forced to look on as other locations and particularly Swindon, developed in leaps and bounds, in consequence of improved communications. Their town was seemingly stagnant, for now with the railway as competition the longer distance mail coaches no longer ran, replaced by a horse drawn vehicle locally referred to as 'Jerry 'Ammond's Bus' and operated by a Mr.Hammond of the *Castle and Ball Hotel*. A contemporary record of a journey in this bus from Swindon to

Marlborough over the windswept downs runs thus:*the rigours of the coach-roof on a winter's dawn when a north wind blew over that wild chalk plateau between Halfway House and Ogbourne ... the amazing contempt for time that marked the getting under way in the darkness of that rattling chariot, which, between the decay of coaching and the extension of the railroad, formed the chief connecting link between Marlborough and Swindon Station; the musty smell of the straw-littered floor and time-worn velvet seats*

As the name suggests, the Kennet and Avon canal provided a link between the rivers of the same name, its course taking the waterway five miles south of Marlborough near the southernmost edge of Savernake Forest. Near a point with the Marlborough - Salisbury coach road a wharf was established, the location taking the name of Burbage. At last then an easier method of transporting coal and other goods to the town had arrived, though offset against this was the relative slowness of water transport generally and the difficult journey between Burbage and Marlborough caused by the steep track through Savernake Forest.Consequently only minor benefits accrued to both canal company and the Town. The waterways prime objective, of course, was the transportation of goods between Bristol and London and there is little reference to the carrying of passenger traffic.

The stage coaches were at first little affected by the new waterway, although it may be assumed not so the pack-horse routes that plied the same course. History fails to provide further details on this aspect.

The greatest change wrought upon the coaching traffic was the opening of the Great Western route through Swindon, the stagecoach passengers being lost to the railway forever. Accordingly business at *The Castle Inn* declined, with speculation as to the fate which might befall the property. Coinciding with the decline of the Inn in its original role, the Rev. Charles Plater had the idea 'to found a school in the area for the education of the sons of gentlefolk' in a fashion similar to the public schools. Support for this scheme was readily forthcoming and accordingly Plater was able to secure a lease on the property with work commencing in 1842 to convert the premises ready for its new role.

The initial intake of Mulburians took place on 23rd August 1843, no less than 200 pupils. The first Master was the Rev.Matthew Wilkinson, late of Clare Hall, Cambridge. Within five years the number of scholars was second only to that of Eton, but unlike the latter, Marlborough was nowhere near as financially secure and there followed a period of difficulty. This did little to endear the pupils to the school and vice versa.

Such problems however were gradually overcome and from then the school has gained a valued reputation as one of the finest in the land. It has also expanded much over the years, the original *Castle Inn* forming part of what is now 'C' house.

Contemporary practice dictated that at first only two terms were necessary per calendar year. However, this was later changed in favour of the more conventional arrangement familiar now. A few years later the advent of the branch railway allowed scholars to avail themselves of the new form of transport and some fascinating running of 'special college trains' will be discussed fully later on.

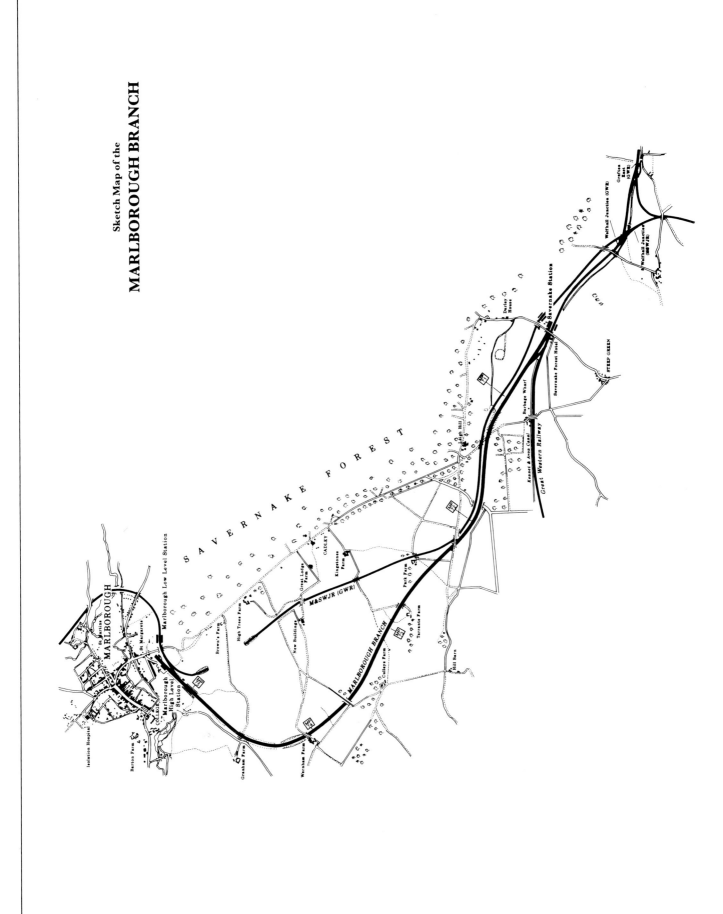

Sketch Map of the

MARLBOROUGH BRANCH

CHAPTER THREE

A RAILWAY AT LAST

The Act of Parliament authorising construction of the Marlborough Railway was passed on 22nd. July 1861. This allowed for the building of a 5½ mile line from the Berks and Hants Extension Railway at what was later to be Savernake Station, to the town of Marlborough. However, despite the obvious recorded existence of dates and facts of similar ilk, there is a distinct lack of reference to the Company's early history, prior to 1861. The reader's indulgence is then requested in attempting to piece together a jig-saw with many missing pieces.

Some of these gaps are explained in an unusual way. The promoters of the Marlborough line were mostly the influential citizens and landowners of the area and who, it would appear, conducted much of their own business at meetings other than official Marlborough Railway work. Of course legal requirements stipulated that a certain number of directors and shareholders meetings should be held, and indeed records from the vast majority of these have survived; but the gaps referred to above are nevertheless still present.

Arguably foremost in support for a railway to the town was the Rev. J.S.Thomas, Bursar of Marlborough College from 1860 - 1897. It was he who rallied other influential persons in the area including Jonah Reeve (the Mayor), James Blake Maurice and F.J.Leader, all of whom were well known individuals. The first published reference to the project appears in *The Marlborough Times* of 19th November 1859. This indicated the intention to apply to Parliament for powers to build a railway, ironically without giving the name of the promoters. On 21st. December 1859 a public meeting was held in the Town Hall with the definite purpose of rallying support for the project. The chair was taken by Mayor Reeve. *The Marlborough Times* in its report of the proceedings quoted an interview with a Mr. Manning, a London solicitor:

The present project had its origin in an interview with Lord Ernest Bruce on the occasion of the turning of the first sod of the Andover & Redbridge Railway by Lord Palmerston. The proposed branch would form a junction at Burbage with the Berks and Hants Extension Railway and with the Andover and Redbridge Extension Railway.

Support for a railway to Marlborough was certainly forthcoming from the businessmen of the area, who were concerned to see their Town connected to the national railway network. Apart from the financial aspect they gave little thought to how or where it might be done. The nearest connection that could be made was with the Berks and Hants Extension line, some 5½ miles south and at this stage the idea of a 12 mile line between Marlborough and Swindon was some way in the future. A Bill for powers to construct a railway from Savernake to Marlborough was thus entered for Parliament in the session for 1860 and with success seemingly assured.

It was probably around this time that a successful approach was made to the Marquess of Ailesbury to become chairman of the venture. Indeed the support of this individual was crucial to the project as the family were major landowners on the route of the projected railway. The title Ailesbury was first conferred upon Charles Brundell Bruce, who had previously been known as Viscount Savernake, in 1821. The second Marquess, and the son of Charles Bruce, took the same title upon the death of his father in 1856, whilst in addition succeeding his cousin to the title as the eighth Earl of Cardigan. Upon his death in 1878 another son, Ernest Augustus Charles Bruce, acceded to administer the title and Tottenham House, the family home, as well as the estate at Savernake. It was Earnest Bruce then - later the Third Marquess - who is referred to above as being associated with the railway. To further complicate matters, Earnest Bruce was sometimes referred to as the Rt.Hon. Lord Earnest Bruce M.P.

The Marquess is worthy of further mention at this early stage, for with the Bruce family as owners of much of Savernake Forest together with tracts of adjacent land they had already been involved with the Kennet & Avon Canal Company and Berks and Hants Extension Railway, both of which traversed the estate. The family having been a successful influence in the fortunes of both endeavours, the Marlborough Railway was almost assured success from the start, a situation which many other small lines would no doubt have envied. (The key stone to the east arch of the canal tunnel under the railway at Savernake still bears the inscription of Lord Bruce and has always been officially known as the Bruce Tunnel).

Other than the involvement of the Rev. Thomas, Marlborough College took little part in the proceedings, for despite maintaining a strong influence both in the town and the district, little land belonging to the College was required for the scheme.

The first proposal for a line from Marlborough to Savernake envisaged a connection with both the Berks & Hants Extension and Andover - Redbridge extension lines. At the time the Andover & Redbridge company were attempting to play off the GWR and LSWR against each other and using the tempter of their northwards extension offered the GWR a broad gauge line to within 3 miles of Southampton. But the GWR were cautious in taking the bait, for should they fail and the LSWR wrest control of the northwards extension, there loomed the spectre of a narrow gauge line to Burbage. Part of this fear was based upon the ill defined but quite real territorial boundary separating the Great Western and South Western companies.

Accordingly strong opposition from the GWR in Parliament succeeded in blocking the north - south Andover & Redbridge Extension proposal although in the process the GWR thus lost the opportunity of reaching Southampton via the Andover & Redbridge. The Marlborough branch proposal was itself defeated by the B&H Extension Co. at the same time though surprisingly the minute books of the Company contain no reference to this failing.

At first this opposition by the GWR would appear strange although when analysing such behaviour the reasons become more clear. The GWR at one moment seemed to have the chance of working a line with independent access to the South Coast but could also see the threat of a rival line along much the same course as the former Manchester - Southampton. Had the A & R extension not been defeated then, the South Western would have been poised for even greater success. The GWR no doubt desired to stamp out any opposition by effectively crushing all possible threats; but why still object to the Marlborough branch? On this matter it is impossible now to be precise - possibly the fear was that the two projected lines would form an alliance, such a conclusion attracting weight when in the next breath the GWR offered to support a line to Marlborough, if such a proposal were entered in Parliament for the next session. Is this then partly why the GWR and Marlborough Companies fostered such good relations in later years, the GWR wishing to make up for its behaviour at this time? Probably unlikely, for as hinted at earlier, one attribute the GWR was not renowned for was compassion when dealing with smaller lines. Ironically it was only a decade or so before the Swindon, Marlborough and Andover, later to be the M&SWJ, came upon the scene with a proposal for a line right through the heart of Great Western territory. This time (see for instance *The Midland & South Western Junction Railway*, Bartholomew, Wild Swan) the rival scheme was successful. The histories of the Marlborough Company and M & SWJ were destined to interweave for many years.

To return to 1860; with the defeat of the original railway proposal, no time was lost in preparing an alternative scheme which was little, if at all, altered from the original route. True to

its word, no opposition was encountered from the GWR or Berks and Hants Extension; indeed both companies announced they would promote the Bill, with the GWR agreeing to subscribe £10,000 of the required capital.

The route of the branch had been surveyed by Richard James Ward who was appointed Engineer to the Marlborough Railway Company at an annual salary of £40. Ward, a former pupil of Brunel who was also engineer to the Berks and Hants Extension Co. proposed a route from Savernake Forest station. It would run west around the forest, curving north to terminate in a field with the delightful name of Cherry Orchard, just to the south of the town. In this way the natural obstruction of Savernake Forest would be avoided along with the need for any tunnel, though to compensate for this much of the course involved heavy earthworks and a ruling gradient of less than 1 in 60. Ward's suggestions were accepted by the Directors.

No doubt in some way due to the support of Lord Bruce, shares in the venture were eagerly snapped up. A statistical analysis of ordinary shareholders reveals that of a total of 121 subscribers, all but one had an address in the local area.

Capital for the venture was set at £45,000, the usual additional third, namely £15,000 able to be raised in loans once the whole of the shares had been subscribed to and at least half of the capital paid up.

In what would appear to be a private contact, Lord Bruce as Chairman of the Marlborough Company, together with two of the directors, Henry Bingham Baring, M.P. and Richard Edmonds Price, made contact with the Great Western. The result was a preliminary agreement dated 31st December 1860 for working the new line. A 999 year lease was concluded with arrangements for the GWR to maintain the works after the usual first year. (It was practice for the contractor to look after the works for the first 12 months though as yet of course none had been appointed). Confirmation of the GWR £10,000 subscription to the venture was included in clause 6 of the agreement. Another interesting feature was the standard charge of £750 which the GWR were to pay to the MR annually, in addition to a proportion of receipts.

Interestingly there is no mention, either at this stage or subsequently, of the Marlborough Company giving consideration to the use of their own locomotives and rolling stock.

No time was lost in holding a further public meeting to explain recent developments; this took place at the Town Hall on 1st January 1861 although tantalisingly no report of it survives. It may be safely concluded, however, that support was favourable, allowing for the proposed Bill to be submitted to Parliament. As recounted at the start of the chapter, the Marlborough Railway Bill received the Royal Assent in July the same year.

It would be reasonable to assume therefore that with an Act obtained, and a considerable amount of public support towards the venture, matters could be put in hand almost at once. But instead they appear to have remained dormant for over a year until stirred into activity once more by Rev. Thomas. At a public meeting he pointed out that the best chance of getting the line built on reasonable terms was whilst Messrs. Smith & Knight, the contractors for the Berks & Hants Extension, still had their men and equipment in the neighbourhood. A committee of townspeople was set up and enough capital raised for the venture to begin in earnest.

The directors of the MR therefore approached Smith & Knight with the result that an offer was made by Mr. John Knight (Junior) of Newbury to construct the railway, exclusive of the station at Marlborough, for £33,000.... 'The line to be of single track and to the broad gauge'.

Following on from this, a *memorandum* was sent from the Mayor to the directors of the Berks & Hants Extension Railway

BOROUGH OF
MARLBOROUGH.

Having received a requisition to the effect following :

"As the opening of the Berks and Hants Extension Railway is fixed to take place on the 4th of November next, We, the undersigned, request you to call a Meeting of the Inhabitants, on some early day, to consider what steps can be taken to carry into effect the Act of Parliament which has been obtained, authorizing the making a Branch Railway to Marlborough."

I hereby convene a Meeting of the Inhabitants of the Borough, and other persons interested, to be holden at the Guildhall,

On Thursday, the 23rd of October, inst.,

AT TWELVE O'CLOCK AT NOON.

E. LAWRENCE,
Mayor.

18th October, 1862.

A. EMBERLIN, PRINTER, MARLBOROUGH.

in an effort to enlist their support:

I beg to bring formally to your notice our effort now being made to construct a line of railway for connecting Marlborough with the Berks and Hants Extension by means of a junction at the Savernake Forest Station. The effort has for its object the replacing as far as may be a scheme which suffered defeat in Parliament upon the Petition of your Company.

The Particulars of this proposed undertaking are no doubt well known to you it is therefore almost superfluous to state that an Act of Parliament has been obtained authorising the construction of the Marlborough line and that a considerable proportion of the capital fixed by that Act has already been subscribed for.

Inasmuch as the Branch Railway would most advantageously affect the traffic of the Berks and Hants Extension I hope that I may successfully press upon your attention and request a favourable consideration of the feeling which is generally entertained that your Company will subscribe for shares towards the completion of the communication with Marlborough. I have the honour to be my Lords and Gentlemen, your most obedient and humble servant,

D.P.Maurice, Mayor of Marlborough.

Shortly afterwards the first recorded meeting of the Marlborough Railway Directors occurred. This was held on 5th December 1862 at the home of Mr. Baring. (One may assume the said gentleman was also now a director, although the only new name to come to light at this time is that of W.H. Wilson, the Company Secretary.)

At this meeting it is known that the original offer of £33,000 for the cost of construction rendered by Knight was discussed although this was at variance with Ward's own estimate which he put at £35,525. Ward also submitted his views as to the amount of work necessary:

220,000 cu.yds.	excavation
2,400 cu.yds.	masonry
240 cu.ft.	timber
4 tons.	wrought iron
10	accommodation crossings

The directors for their part made reference to raising the required monies:

£7,500 by local subscription
£10,000 from the GWR
£15,000 in borrowing powers

£1,000 it was hoped, would be invested by the Berks & Hants Extension Co.

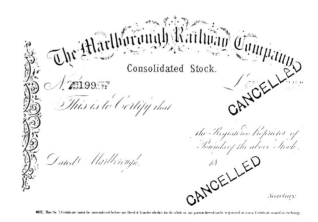

ANNO VICESIMO QUARTO & VICESIMO QUINTO

VICTORIÆ REGINÆ.

****

Cap. clxvɪɪ.

An Act to authorize the Construction of a Railway from the *Berks* and *Hants Extension* Railway to *Marlborough* in *Wiltshire*.　　[22d *July* 1861.]

WHEREAS by "The *Berks and Hants Extension* Railway Act, 1859," the *Berks and Hants Extension* Railway Company were authorized to make a Railway from the *Newbury and Hungerford* Branch of the *Great Western* Railway at *Hungerford* to the *Devizes* Branch of the *Wilts, Somerset, and Weymouth* Railway at *Devizes,* and the Railway so authorized is in the course of Construction: And whereas the making of a Railway from the said *Berks and Hants Extension* Railway to the Town of *Marlborough* in *Wiltshire* would be attended with great local and public Advantage: And whereas the estimated Expense of the said Railway is Forty-five thousand Pounds, and the Persons herein-after named, with others, are willing at their own Expense to construct the Railway: And whereas a Plan and Section of the Railway showing the Line and Levels thereof, with a Book of Reference to the Plan containing the Names of the Owners and Lessees, or reputed Owners and Lessees, and of the Occupiers of the Lands through which the said Railway will pass, have been deposited with the Clerk of the Peace for the said County: And whereas the *Great Western* Railway Company have agreed to work the said *Berks and Hants Extension* Railway when completed, and it is expedient that they should have Power to enter into the Arrangements herein-after contained with respect to the Working and Management of the Railway by this Act authorized, and also to subscribe towards its Construction; but the

22 & 23 Vict. c. cv.

[*Local.*]　　　　　　27 *L*　　　　　　Purposes

14

On that basis the amount to be raised would appear to cover Knight's estimate, although the same minutes contradict this assumption. They record Knight's proposal as worth £38,300 with the proviso that he be prepared to accept £15,000 in shares with the balance in cash. There would appear to be no explanation for these differences.

Leading on from this, several questions immediately come to light, not least of which is the apparent lack of estimates from other contractors! In addition, why the discrepancy between Knight's estimates? More relevant still is the fact that in order to fund the construction the Directors would appear to be placing considerable reliance upon borrowing. In proportion little in the way of the necessary finance was raised by investment, hardly the ideal method of starting the business of running a railway. No mention of an agreed time limit for completion of the works is given.

For reasons that are not completely clear, Knight's tender of £38,300 was accepted, with the formal agreement for construction signed on 20th March 1863. Work began almost at once and without ceremony of any sort. (Even so confusion still arises, for a surviving specification quotes the contract price as £42,000 including stations. Might the difference of £3,700 be 'applicable to the stations'? An exclusion clause allowed the MR to enter a separate contract with another party for the stations if they wished. The reference to stations in the plural is again unexplained).

The same specification also contains a delightful contemporary quote:

The Contractor will at all times during the progress of the works take all requisite precautions and use his best endeavours for preventing all riotous and unlawful behaviour by or amongst the Labourers Workmen and others employed on the Works and for the preservation of the peace and protection of the inhabitants and the security of property in the neighbourhood of the works and will repay all expenses of the Company in respect of any Police or other Peace Officers whom any Justice or Justice of the Peace or other authority shall see fit from time to time to employ in reference to any such behaviour or for such preservation or protection........

Ward was able to report to the Directors on 23rd March 1863 that work on the line had commenced at several points and commented that already 15,000 cu.yds. of excavation had been achieved along with a start made on the principal public road bridge over the Salisbury Turnpike. With the dates of the signing of the contract and the directors meeting obtained from the contemporary documents this would appear to indicate considerable achievement within a very short time.

By May 1863 good progress was still being reported, the directors having decided to obtain outside tenders for the construction of the Marlborough Station buildings. Of these the tender submitted by Messrs. Dalrymple & Findley from Kidlington, Oxford was accepted. This was for £1,867 and included the building of the engine house. (The final cost of this work is believed to have been £2,011 3s. 3d, whilst the name of the contractors is also referred to as Dabrymple & Finlay.)

In September of the same year Ward was able to report 166,000 cu. yds. of excavation work, with completion hoped for by the end of November ..... *The bridges either finished or in an advanced state and the permanent way commenced at Savernake. The junction with the main line was also completed and the signals altered to suit the working of the branch..... In relation to the station contract; .....the station building is making good progress with the engine house walls half finished..... He concluded by adding.....the permanent way fittings for Marlborough Terminus had been ordered by the contractor and were to be delivered in early November.....*

The only reported difficulty encountered was in the cutting between Leigh Hill and Hat Gate where a very hard bed of chalk rock was encountered, which had to be shifted by blasting. The additional work was reported as adding an extra

£4,000 to the cost of construction.

The contract provides some interesting insights as to the required specifications:

Fencing .....*A good and substantial iron wire fence shall be formed on both sides of the railway.....and connected in a good and workmanlike manner with the wing walls of any bridges or other structure or the fences of any roads which may intercept the same and shall be properly and securely fixed to the fence which may be fixed along the top of the slopes of any Road approaches or divisions of Roads formed under for the purpose of this contract. This fence railing is to consist of Hernuleivicry Galvanized wire fencing 2 top wires being No. 0 and the 4 lower wires of the No. 1 strand with Patent winding straining Pillars 200 yards minimum distance apart with intermediate bar iron standards one-and-three-quarter inches by three-eighths inches with double concave earth plates 9 feet apart as shown in drawing No. 2A the whole to be twice painted or Oak or Larch posts of the same scantling and lengths and prepared as on the Aylesbury Branch of the Wycombe Railway.*

Permanent Way .....*The Permanent Way will consist of a single line of Railway, the rails being laid upon pine packing nailed to the longitudinal timbers and fastened down by fangbolts. And with joint plates under the end of the rails and hard wood plugs about 12 inches long filling the hollows of the rails at the joints with the transomes housed and fastened into the longitudinal timbers.....Longitudinals 12 x 6. Sharpbolts, 480 double sets per mile. Rail joint plates, 528 per mile. Rails Bridge Pattern weighing ninety-seven-and-a-half tons per mile or 62 lbs. per yard.*

Ward however was proven to be a little optimistic with regard to his ideal timings for completion of the work. Not until 18th January 1864 was official notification sent from Wilson, the MR Co. Secretary to the Board of Trade, giving the statutory one month's notice of opening. This was followed on 25th February by a further letter stating the line would be ready for inspection on 7th March. Ballast was obtained from a field near Newbury and possibly near to where Enborne Junction was later sited. This source was used for both the Marlborough and Berks & Hants Extension Company lines.

Wilson had himself been optimistic although no doubt he acted purely on the information supplied to him; on 4th March 1864 a letter was hurriedly sent to the Board of Trade in an attempt to withdraw the earlier notice of 25th February. As far as the Board of Trade was concerned it had been delayed enough and on 8th March 1864 Captain Rich arrived to inspect the new line. As usual the Board of Trade Inspecting Officers' report is a most useful source of contemporary information:

I have the honour to report for the information of the Lords of the Committee of the Priory Council for London that in compliance with your minute of the 4th inst. I have this day inspected the Marlborough Railway.

The new line which is 5m 48ch. long commences at Savernake Station on the Hungerford Branch of the Great Western, and extends thence to Marlborough which is the only other Station on the line.

It is single throughout with sidings at the terminal stations. The passenger trains run in at the back of the present passenger platform at Savernake so as not to interfere with the main line. There are no turntables, so it will be necessary that the Company should undertake to work the line with tank engines only if they do not propose to erect turntables.

The permanent way consists of bridge rail weighing 62 lbs. per crucial yard in lengths of 28ft and 24ft. It is laid on longitudinal sleepers 12ft x 6in tied with transomes 11ft apart. The joints are fastened with fang bolts and laid on iron plates, a hard wood plug being inserted in the hollow part of the rail.

The gauge is 7ft the ballast gravel, chalk and broken stone laid about 1ft deep where complete. There are no public level crossings. The old road marked No. 9 at 1m 58ch has been deviated through the adjacent underbridge. There are 3 underbridges constructed of brick and a fourth of wrought iron girders.

Two overbridges are built of brick and a third has wrought iron girders.

24° & 25° VICTORIÆ, *Cap.*clxvii

The Marlborough Railway Act, 1861

MARLBOROUGH RAILWAY, 5½ MILES (CHARGED AS 6).

SCALE of DIVISION of TRAFFIC, with a minimum Rate of 50 and a maximum Rate of 60 per Cent. to the Great Western Railway Company, after Deduction of 750*l.* per Annum.

WHEN THE TRAFFIC SHALL BE

	At and under 15*l.* per Mile per Week.		At 16*l.* per Mile per Week.		At 17*l.* per Mile per Week.		At 18*l.* per Mile per Week.		At 19*l.* per Mile per Week.		At 20*l.* per Mile per Week.		At 21*l.* per Mile per Week.		At 22*l.* per Mile per Week.		At 23*l.* per Mile per Week.		At 24*l.* per Mile per Week.		At and over 25*l.* per Mile per Week.	
	Per Cent.		Per Cent.		Per Cent.		Per Cent.		Per Cent.		Per Cent.		Per Cent.		Per Cent.		Per Cent.		Per Cent.		Per Cent.	
Gross Receipts per Annum - -		4680		4992		5304		5616		5928		6240		6552		6864		7176		7488		7800
Deduct - - -		750		750		750		750		750		750		750		750		750		750		750
Balance divisible -		3930		4242		4554		4866		5178		5490		5802		6114		6426		6738		7050
To Marlborough Company - -	50	1965	49	2079	48	2186	47	2287½	46	2383	45	2472½	44	2553	43	2630	42	2701	41	2766	40	2820
and To Great Western Railway Company	50	1965	51	2163	52	2368	53	2578½	54	2795	55	3017½	56	3249	57	3484	58	3725	59	3972	60	4230

LONDON:

Printed by GEORGE EDWARD EYRE and WILLIAM SPOTTISWOODE.

Printers to the Queen's most Excellent Majesty. 1861.

The whole of these works appear to be substantially constructed and of sufficient strength. A brick underbridge near Marlborough is slightly bulged and not of shape, but this appears to be caused from imperfect building rather than any subsequent failure.

The heavy embankment at each side of this bridge is not yet sufficiently consolidated. It gave in places considerably under the engine.

The fencing on the north side of the line from this bridge to the next cutting is also incomplete. Chock blocks are required at all the sidings and indicators to the facing points at Marlborough.

These works can all be finished in a few days and the embankment if properly cured and ballasted with one engine will probably consolidate in 10 days or a fortnight, but I am of the opinion that in its present state the Marlborough Railway cannot be opened for passenger traffic without danger to the public using the service.

I have received no undertakings as to the proposed mode of working.

Capt. Rich obviously had the use of an engine to conduct his inspection but this was not the first train to traverse the full length of the line. A few days previously, on 2nd March a special had arrived at the terminus conveying the GWR Superintendent from Reading, Mr. Bailey, along with a Mr. Codrington, also of the GWR. Whatever Ward as Engineer to the MR may have thought at the failure to obtain sanction for the opening is not recorded. Instead he reported to the directors on 22nd March 1864 that the line was complete, '.....apart from a few unimportant details'..... Referring to the Board of Trade Inspection he continued ..... *The Government Inspector examined the line on the 8th inst. and expressed satisfaction with the works but recommended that the opening should be deferred for a short time in order that the heavy newly formed embankment should have time to consolidate. In that recommendation, I entirely concur.*

Evidently the directors either had complete faith in their engineer or they were preoccupied with other matters to realise exactly what had taken place. Probably a bit of both, for at the time they had before them a letter from the GWR as to the proposed fares:

1st Class Single 1/2d. (All refer to Marlborough - Savernake)
2nd Class Single 10d.
3rd Class Single 5½d

1st Class Return 1/9d
2nd Class Return 1/3d

There was no rate for a 3rd class return listed. Ward's report was passed without further comment.

At the same meeting the directors wrote to the GWR refusing to purchase the required furniture for Marlborough station. Instead they commented.....*if the GWR not being satisfied the question must be referred as provided for under the provision of the Agreement, in the meantime the GWR can supply the articles required without prejudice* ..... Fighting talk indeed for such a small company against the might of the GWR, yet they apparently

succeeded, for nothing else is heard of the matter.

Just a few days later on 26th March 1864 the necessary work referred to by Capt. Rich was reported as completed and a request for an immediate reinspection of the line was made. Unfortunately at that time another of the Board of Trade Inspectors, Colonel Yolland, was ill and with Captain Rich busy on additional work the reinspection was delayed. Four days elapsed before Capt. Rich again visited the line, on 30th March, with local legend recalling that on this occasion it was necessary for some of the passengers in the inspection train to get out and push - shades of *The Titfield Thunderbolt*. This time Capt. Rich found all his objections attended to. He did nevertheless comment further that the edge of the platform at Marlborough was too close to the rails, and should be 2ins further back. Ward agreed to see to this and without further difficulty the line was passed as fit for use.

But it had been a close run thing, Capt. Rich conducting his inspection in nothing other than the *inaugural train* from Savernake to Marlborough arranged by the directors. The GWR does not seem to have helped matters much, providing '.....no more nor less than an old ballast engine.....', which stalled several times on the trip.

At the ceremonial luncheon that followed, the health of the Inspector was toasted. *The Marlborough Times* records Captain Rich returning the honour as follows:

If all present patronise it (the railway) as they ought, I have no doubt that the dividends and everything else will be satisfactory. I hope you will have something better for an engine to carry you, not to be stopped midway, but that was from no fault in the line. It was not the curves nor the gradients, for I have inspected lines with much greater, but the incapacity of the engine, which was nothing more or less than an old ballast engine, not quite equal to the work.

The final stage in preparation for the public service occurred the following day, 31st March. A sealed undertaking forwarded by the Marlborough Railway to the Board of Trade stated that the line would only be worked by 'one engine and train' and the way was thus clear for public services to begin, although at this time no official commencement date was given.

Lord Bruce was later able to announce the imminent opening of the railway, although before this took place one man at least, intending to travel to Savernake came to Marlborough from nearby Avebury only to find the service not yet started. Why there should have been this delay is unclear, for the Directors would have wished to operate trains and thereby accrue revenue as soon as possible. Perhaps the answer lies with the Great Western, as on 12th April 1864 a new contract .....*as to the use and working of the Marlborough Railway*..... was signed by the two concerns. Like before, this was to run for 999 years. The division of receipts is otherwise identical to the earlier 1860 agreement.

SIX PER CENT PREFERENCE SHARE.

The Marlborough Railway Company

INCORPORATED BY 24th & 25th VICTORIA, CAP. 167.

Certificate of £10. Share.

[PAID IN FULL.]

This is to Certify that ..... is the Proprietor of the Preference Share of Ten Pounds No. 500 in the Marlborough Railway Company issued under the authority of The Marlborough Railway (Additional Capital) Certificate 1868, with a Preferential Dividend of Six Pounds per contum per annum, in priority of all existing and future Shares or Stock of the Company subject to the Rules and Regulations of the Company.

Given under the Common Seal of the Company the 1st day of January 1870.

W. H. Wilson   Secretary

(Policy of Resolutions on the other side)

40 June, 1865.

BRANCH LINES.

LONDON, READING, & NEWBURY, HUNGERFORD, DEVIZES, & TROWBRIDGE, To BATH, BRISTOL, SALISBURY, and WEYMOUTH.

Distance from Paddington	DOWN. Starting from		Week Days. 1 & 2 class. a.m.	1 & 2 class. a.m.	1, 2, 3 class. a.m.	1 & 2 class. a.m.	1 & 2 class. p.m.	Exp. 1 & 2 class p.m.	Sundays. 1, 2, 3 class. a.m.	1 & 2 class. p.m.	
—	London	Paddington	.	.	7 5	10 25	3 40	6 15	9 0	4 45	.
		Victoria	.	..	..	9 55	2 0	..	8 35	4 0	..
		Kensington	...	...	...	10 18	2 20	...	8 54	4 20	...
—	Windsor	.	.	.	7 20	11 0	3 5	5 45	9 35	5 15	.
—	Oxford	.	...	..	7 25	9 30	2 20	5 0	6 55	4 10	..
36	Reading	...	.	.	8 50	12 0	4 38	7 5	10 40	6 15	.
41¼	Theale	.	..	..	9 3	12 12	4 50	7 17	10 52	6 28	..
44¾	Aldermaston	..	...	...	9 12	12 20	4 58	7 24	11 0	6 36	...
46¾	Woolhampton	...	.	.	9 18	12 26	5 4	7 30	11 6	6 42	.
49½	Thatcham	.	..	..	9 26	12 33	5 12	7 37	11 13	6 50	..
53	Newbury	..	...	...	9 40	12 44	5 22	7 47	11 22	7 0	...
58½	Kintbury	...	.	.	9 53	12 56	5 35	7 59	11 34	7 13	.
61¼	Hungerford	.	..	..	10 3	1 5	5 42	8 7	11 40	7 22	..
56¾	Bedwyn	..	...	...	10 17	1 20	5 55	8 18	11 55	7 37	...
70	Savernake	...	.	.	10 27	1 30	6 3	8 27	12 5	7 47	.
75¼	Marlborough	dep.	.	.	10 10	1 5	5 45	.	.	.	.
		arr.	..	..	10 50	1 50	6 43	..	..	..	..
75½	Pewsey	.	..	..	10 40	1 40	6 15	8 40	12 18	8 0	..
79	Woodborough	..	...	...	10 50	1 50	6 25	8 50	12 27	8 10	...
86	Devizes	Arr	.	.	11 5	2 5	6 40	9 3	12 40	8 25	
		Dep	7 25	9 0	11 15	2 10	7 5	9 10	p.m. 12 45	.	.
90¼	Seend	.	7 35	9 10	11 25	..	7 15	..	12 55	..	..
94¼	Holt Junction	..	...	9 20	...	...	...	...	...	...	...
97¾	Trowbridge	Arr	7 55	9 35	11 45	2 40	7 35	9 35	1 15	.	.
110	Bath	.	8 55		12 35	3 45	8 35	10 10	1 55	..	..
121½	Bristol	..	9 35	...	1 5	4 25	9 5	10 40	2 25	...	...
197	Exeter	...	12 45	.	Cl.1&2 4 15	8 10	a.m. 3 10	.	6 45	.	.
249¾	Plymouth	.	3 55	..	7 15	11 55	5 25	..	9 50	..	..
97½	Trowbridge, for Salisbury	Dep	8 5	.	11 50	2 35	7 40	.	6 40	.	.
126	Salisbury ...	Arr	9 30	..	1 35	4 10	9 20	..	8 35	..	..
97½	Trowbridge, for Weymouth	Dep	8 0	.	12 15	2 45	7 55	.	6 45	.	.
106¾	Frome	.	8 40	..	12 37	3 12	8 20	..	7 10	..	..
132¾	Yeovil	..	9 45	...	1 35	4 10	9 10	...	8 10	...	...
153½	Dorchester	...	10 35	.	2 15	5 5	9 50	.	9 5	.	.
169½	Weymouth	Arr	10 50		2 30	5 20	10 5	..	9 20	..	..

Distance from Weymouth	UP. Starting from		Week Days. 1 & 2 class. a.m.	1 & 2 class. a.m.	1 & 2 class. a.m.	1, 2, 3 class. a.m.	1 & 2 class. p.m.	1 & 2 class. p.m.		Sundays. 1, 2, 3 class. a.m.	1 & 2 class. a.m.
—	Weymouth, for Trowbridge	Dep	.	6 0	*Via Chippenham.*	9 0	12 50	12 50	.	.	9 30
7	Dorchester	..	..	6 15		9 17	1 5	1 5	..	...	9 50
27½	Yeovil	...	...	6 55		10 10	1 45	1 45	...	...	10 40
53¼	Frome	.	.	7 53		11 20	2 40	2 40	.	.	11 38
63	Trowbridge	Arr	..	8 15		11 55	3 5	3 5	..	...	12 0
			Express from Reading.	C							
83½	Salisbury, fr Trowbridge	Dep		6 50		10 25	1 40	1 40	.	.	8 5
63	Trowbridge	Arr		8 20		12 0	3 10	3 10	..	..	9 25
215¾	Plymouth	Dep		.		.	6 45	a.m. 10 45	.	.	6 45
162¼	Exeter	..		..		7 35	9 45	12 53	..	..	10 0
87¼	Bristol	...		6 50	8 40	10 45	1 25	3 55	...	...	3 30
76	Bath	.		7 25	9 10	11 10	1 55	4 25	.	.	4 5
63	Trowbridge	Dep		8 22	9 50	12 10	3 15	5 10	..	..	4 45
66	Holt Junction	...		8 30	10 15	12 20	3 25	5 20	...	...	4 55
70	Seend	.		.	10 30	12 30	3 35	5 30	.	.	5 5
74¼	Devizes	Arr		8 47	10 45	12 45	3 50	5 40	..	..	5 20
		Dep	7 30	8 50	.	12 50	.	5 50	.	8 30	5 25
81¼	Woodborough	..	7 43	H	..	1 5	..	6 5	..	8 41	5 40
85¾	Pewsey	...	7 51	9 6	...	1 15	...	6 15	...	8 52	5 50
91¼	Marlborough	dep.	.	8 55	.	1 5	.	5 45	.	.	.
		arr.	..	9 40	..	1 50	..	6 43	..	..	..
90¼	Savernake	.	8 5	9 18	.	1 30	.	6 28	.	9 5	6 3
93¾	Bedwyn	..	8 15	..	..	1 40	..	6 36	..	9 15	6 13
99	Hungerford	...	8 30	9 32	...	1 55	...	6 50	...	9 30	6 30
102	Kintbury	.	8 36	.	.	2 3	.	6 57	.	9 37	6 37
108	Newbury	..	8 45	9 47	..	2 20	..	7 10	..	9 50	6 50
111	Thatcham	...	8 53	...	...	2 30	...	7 18	...	9 58	7 0
113¾	Woolhampton	.	8 59	.	.	2 38	.	7 24	.	10 5	7 8
115¾	Aldermaston	..	9 5	10 0	..	2 44	..	7 30	..	10 11	7 14
119¾	Theale	...	9 13	10 7	...	2 54	...	7 38	...	10 20	7 23
124½	Reading	Arr	9 30	10 20	..	3 10	.	7 50	.	10 35	7 40
—	Oxford	Arr	11 0	11 10	.	5 30	.	9 40	.	11 45	9 47
—	Windsor	.	10 47	11 55	..	3 57	..	9 7	..	3 0	8 52
160¾	London	Kensingtn	...	12 37	...	...	...	...	...	3 22	.
		Victoria	.	12 55	.	.	.	.	.	3 40	..
		Paddingtn	10 25	11 15	..	4 15	..	9 0	..	3 15	9 40

H Carriages and Horses are not conveyed by this Train.

C Salisbury Passengers by this Train change carriages at Westbury, and by all the other Trains at Trowbridge. Weymouth Passengers change carriages at Trowbridge.

Commencing then on 14th April 1864 the first public train service consisted of five trains each way daily. The journey time was scheduled at 15 minutes, an average speed of just under 22 m.p.h. Two of the trains ran 'mixed' and there was no Sunday service. The locomotives and stock for the line were provided by the Great Western from the outset.

of the company to place all the available shares. Costs involved in constructing the railway had indeed been high, exceeding the available capital, even allowing for maximum use of the borrowing powers authorised by the 1861 Act. As an example the figures for the capital account as at 31.12.1867 read as follows:

Down	Mixed	Pass	Mixed	Pass	Pass
Savernake.dep.	9.30am	10.35am	1.35pm	6.28pm	8.30pm
Marlboro.arr.	9.45am	10.50am	1.50pm	6.43pm	8.45pm
Up	Pass	Pass	Mixed	Pass	Pass
Marlboro.dep.	9.10am	10.10am	1.05pm	5.35pm	8.05pm
Savernake.arr.	9.25am	10.25am	1.20pm	5.50pm	8.20pm

Adequate connections with the main line services in both directions were sensibly provided. A similar timetable was in use the following year.

The leisurely schedule however brought forth caustic comments from some quarters. An early postcard depicted the 'Marlborough Donkey' against which was the following quote.....*You may push and you may shove, But I'm hanged if I'll be druv*..... It is possible that this was intended to refer as well to the events of the inspection on 30th March *ultimo*.

By comparison with the main line, where there were only four trains each way the branch was nevertheless better off and despite any misgivings receipts were, at least at the outset, fairly promising.

The opening of the railway was reported to the Directors at the Board meeting of 2nd May 1864. The same meeting is known to have referred to the costs accrued to date although figures are unfortunately not recorded.

Information on the first few years from 1864 -1868 is generally scant, though the occasional tantalising glimpse is given. One instance occurs at the Board meeting of 13th October 1864, with a passing reference to the proposed extension from Marlborough to Calne, but nothing else is heard of this. Calne itself had been served by its own branch from Chippenham since 3rd November 1863 and so it was unlikely that the project would find much favour. The town of Calne is some 13 miles from Marlborough along the old coaching road, now known as the A4, and it was by this route that a horse bus ran, connecting the two localities. It is believed to have started at the same time as the Marlborough Railway, whilst the GWR later had a road motor service between the two towns, as described elsewhere in this account.

Despite the lack of information during the first few years one thing is certain, that no dividends were at first paid. More than two and a half years after opening, receipts still only yielded £6 per mile weekly.

Much of this financial difficulty had been due to the inability

Original Capital Authorised	£45000.00.00
Borrowing Authorised	£15000.00.00*

Situation at 31st December 1867 (shares taken up)

1st call, £2.10 Jan 1863	£ 4592.10.00
2nd call, £3 May 1863	£ 5475.00.00
3rd call, £2 Aug 1863	£ 3334.00.00
4th call, £2.10 Feb.1864	£ 4152.10.00
Contractor	£12580.00.00
	£30134.00.00

£13960 of shares were unissued and there was £906 arrears.

Loans on mortgage debentures	£12815.04.07
Lloyds bond	£ 2046.11.00
Transfer from Revenue Account	£ 54.11.01
	£45950.04.07

Expenditure

Parliamentary Expenses	£ 1386.14.06
Construction Costs	£36437.05.11
Engineers Fees	£ 1300.00.00
Land and compensation	£ 3566.10.00
Station contract	£ 1950.00.00
Interest discount and commissions	£ 855.10.11
Salaries	£ 165.00.00
Printing stationary and miscellaneous	£ 154.18.03
Balance	£ 134.05.00
	£45950.04.07

The Company minute books record that further expenditure would also be required, amounting to just over £5,000 on land, works, law, engineer and sundries, most of this attributable to the extra work made necessary by blasting.

Faced with the prospect of being unlikely to be able to discharge its future liabilities, the company made an approach to the Board of Trade for authorisation to raise up to £6,000 of additional share capital, partly in loan form. This was approved under the title of 'The Marlborough Railway (Additional Capital) Certificate 1868'. It would appear there was little local success in generating extra support, for at the meeting of 29th March 1870 the directors reported they had been unsuccessful in placing the shares despite offering a preference dividend of 6%. Consequently, as before, no dividend could be paid on ordinary shares. One can anticipate the feelings then of the ordinary shareholder. General dissension was expected, especially as this was the seventh consecutive year this had happened but surprisingly there appeared to be little disquiet. Official company records in any case show that £4,800, previously issued in preference shares, was held by only five persons, one of whom was allotted £4,000. Regarding the holding of ordinary shares, these were nearly all held by individuals owning between 1 and 100 in quantity, with two obvious exceptions - the contractor and the GWR. Few changes in share ownership appear to have occurred, for of the 141 concerns or individuals holding ordinary shares there were still 120 with an address in the Marlborough area). With the authority of the new 1868 certificate the Company subsequently borrowed £4,000 from Northern Assurance against security of a debenture bond yielding interest at the rate of 5% per annum.

From what would appear then to have been a precarious start matters began to improve dramatically, the ensuing years seeing a rise in receipts and consequently dividends so that those who had failed to invest originally were left regretting their decision. Not all of this was due to the management of the company. A considerable amount of credit must be laid at the door of others, notably the GWR who successfully manipulated the little company throughout the the next 25 years.

At this early time, for reasons not wholly clear, receipts on the branch began to improve, and from mid-1869 onwards, although receipts for the half year are credited at £1803.8.6d this is not immediately apparent from the traffic returns. Unfortunately it is one of the few occasions when the records convert the numbers of passengers and tonnages, etc. into hard cash.

Accordingly at the half yearly meeting of 28th September 1870 the directors were able to report, ...the placing of sufficient numbers of preference shares to provide for the discharge of all the outstanding liabilities of the Company and there now only remain some very small accounts which will be very shortly settled..... A dividend of £1 percent p.a. free of tax was recommended on ordinary shares. Subsequent dividends and reports for the various half years are appended at the end of the chapter.

A minor development occurred in 1871, the moving of the Company office from 6 Victoria Street, Westminster to Marlborough itself. The six monthly shareholders' meetings were now also held in the local Town Hall. In charge of matters locally was a new company secretary Mr. James Leader, replacing W.H. Wilson. Leader's remuneration was fixed at £40 p.a. Presumably this was the same F.J.Leader referred to earlier.

From the spring of 1872 the Great Western introduced additional facilities for third class passengers on the branch, reflected in a dramatic increase in revenue from around this time. A further increase took place when Marlborough College rearranged its existing academic year from two to three terms coupled with facilities for an increased number of pupils. This growing traffic was destined to be short lived and by the end of 1874 receipts had fallen drastically due, it was reported, to a fare increase by the Great Western. It is possible to conclude therefore, that throughout the line's independent days, matters such as rates for travel were fixed by the operating rather than the owning company and without, it would appear, any reference to the latter.

A major change took place in mid-1874, involving the conversion of the line from the broad to the narrow or standard gauge. The GWR had previously given notice that the cost of this was estimated at £2,600, which would be treated as a loan. The Marlborough Company responded by declaring it had neither the funds nor the borrowing powers available and was not prepared for the sake of dividends to borrow the monies at the offered 5% interest. There matters rested seemingly without agreement though behind the scenes a private deal appears to have been struck, for at the Board meeting of 15th June 1874 the directors agreed to bear half the cost of the work, 'provided the whole expense did not exceed £1,500.' This was reported to the shareholders on 30th June 1874. The Marlborough Company were able to borrow the money from the GWR itself at the reduced rate of 4%. A similar arrangement would appear to have been made between the Berks & Hants Extension Co. and the GWR.

The gauge conversion took place from Saturday 27th June 1874 onwards, the first narrow gauge trains running the following Wednesday, 1st July 1874. Sensibly this was the same time schedule as used for conversion of the main line through Savernake. What arrangements were made (if any) for the traffic during this period of temporary closure are unknown.

1870 Service Timetable

Down	Mixed	Pass	Pass	Pass	Pass	Pass
Savernake.dep.	9.10am	10.25am	1.45pm	4.25pm	6.15pm	9.00
Marlborough.arr.	9.25am	10.40am	2.00pm	4.40pm	6.30pm	9.15
Up	**Pass**	**Pass**	**Pass**	**Pass**	**Pass**	**Mixed**
Marlborough.dep.	8.40am	10.10am	12.45pm	4.00pm	5.45pm	7.55
Savernake.arr.	8.55am	10.15am	1.00pm	4.15pm	6.00pm	8.10

Again there was no Sunday service.

Following the gauge conversion there is no mention in official reports of a re-inspection of the branch by the Board of Trade. The only reference from this time describes the track being laid 'on longitudinal baulks.' It was to be three years before the Board of Trade would inspect the revised layout and even then with scant reference to the branch. Further details of this are given in the section on Savernake Station.

Despite uncertainty then as to the cost of the gauge conversion the Company were able to pay off, in full, their loan from the Northern Assurance Co. on 15th July 1874. This is especially interesting as only a few months earlier they had spoken of being unable to raise funds to pay the originally quoted cost of the gauge conversion. The monies were immediately reborrowed from the same source but this time on the slightly more favourable terms of 4½% annually.

THE IMPACT OF THE SWINDON MARLBOROUGH AND ANDOVER RAILWAY

The promotion and subsequent building of the Swindon, Marlborough and Andover Railway without doubt had the biggest effect on the fortunes of the Marlborough branch during its brief history. To quantify this it is first necessary to discuss the fortunes of the SMA from 1873 onwards.

As previously recounted, the idea of a through line linking the north and midlands with the south had been around since the time of *The Railway Mania* back in the 1840s. The ambitious Manchester and Southampton scheme, the one that came closest to fruition, for part of its course followed the path of the later SMA. With the opening of the Marlborough Railway in 1864 and also the Andover to Redbridge (near Southampton) route in 1865, sections of the original Manchester & Southampton scheme were being filled. It did not take long to realise then that a new route joining the various sections was a distinct possibility.

Following several false starts in the 1860s, and mostly because of the opposition of the GWR, a new Bill for a line from Swindon to Marlborough and from Savernake to Andover was proposed in 1873. The GWR amongst others felt there was little chance of it succeeding, primarily due to anticipated opposition from various landowners. With apparently little serious difficulty then the Swindon, Marlborough and Andover Railway Act became law on 21st July 1873.

Much of this success can be fairly laid at the hands of Lord Bruce who besides being Chairman of the existing Marlborough company was also Chairman of the new concern. The immediate impression is that the Marlborough company were delighted with the prospect of additional traffic using their line,

It is a matter of great regret that no photographs appear to have survived showing the Marlborough Branch as broad gauge. Indeed the earliest known view dates from about 1890, though an 1881 photograph of the rival SMA station does survive, clearly showing the new track converging into a single line of rails at the south end of the station, prior to the connection with the Marlborough Railway.

George Lait

for increased revenue would be bound to accrue. Surprisingly, this was not the case. J.C. Townsend, the Marlborough Railway solicitor was only too aware of the opposition the scheme would generate at Paddington and was fearful of the latter's wrath. His fears and objections were overruled by bolder Lord Bruce.

The SMA Act provided for an end-on connection at Marlborough, approached from the north by either a viaduct or 67ft embankment. Necessary for the crossing of the Kennet valley, it explains why the terminus of the Marlborough Railway had been located a short distance from the town. The ruling gradient of the MR was also to be eased from about 1 in 60 to 1 in 90* whilst the line itself would be doubled. The MR was permitted to subscribe up to £25,000 towards the scheme although it is not thought that as a company it ever invested a penny. Running powers by the SMA over the MR and the GWR between the junction at Savernake were included in the Act.

First sod of the SMA was turned in a field at Meddown on 28th July 1875, the town of Marlborough bedecked with flags for the event and displaying far more enthusiasm towards this venture than had ever been so for the MR itself.

Unfortunately, such enthusiasm was not converted into financial backing, and construction work on the SMA ceased in October 1876 due to lack of funds. An approach was then made to the GWR for assistance but for the reasons already outlined this did not meet with any enthusiasm. The directors of the SMA now sought ways of reducing the required expenditure, one of these being a general steepening of gradients which meant that at Marlborough a separate station would be required with a junction into the MR just south of the branch terminus.

Following a successful application to Parliament for an extension of time the directors of the SMA managed to get construction going again. Their contractor Messrs. Watson. Smith & Watson entered into an agreement with the GWR on 21st February 1881......*as to a temporary junction siding and works at the Marlborough Station on the Great Western Company's Railway.....* Of course at this time the MR was still an independent concern and it would be expected that their name would appear upon the title of the agreement. Such omissions were quite a regular occurence, characterising a number of contemporary official documents and giving the impression that the MR were kept very much in the dark by the GWR.

This temporary siding was to assist in bringing materials to Marlborough for use in constructing the SMA, yet it is perhaps surprising that such a facility was only provided a matter of months before the SMA was completed as far as the town. Certainly it is known that materials for the construction had been brought to Marlborough in quantity prior to this and offloaded at the existing station. This is confirmed in the record of the public meeting of the Marlborough company on 22nd March 1882 where, it was reported.....*there has been a decrease in goods traffic by £120.14s.1d compared with 1880, but this had been due to a considerable amount of material carried over the MR during construction of the SMA.....* The SMA route from Swindon to their own Marlborough station was finally opened to the public from 27th July 1881.

At the time there was no physical connection between the two stations at Marlborough and consequently through running was not possible. Similarly the section of SMA route south from Savernake to Andover was still to be opened and no work had yet been undertaken, either easing the gradients or doubling the original line. But that does not mean the MR did not benefit from its new neighbour, for although passengers travelling to and from London now had the choice of two routes it is said receipts on the branch *increased*, although regretfully the figures

to prove this are not available. Other than this the MR are reported to have made a concession with regard to the cost of the cartage of coal and so bring their charges more into line with the SMA. (The MR directors had in fact already received a memorial on the subject of their rates for goods traffic in 1879. It would appear at that time no action was taken.)

Describing the opening of the SMA route of necessity involves a jump ahead in years and we must now return to the 1870s, when the various events are recorded at the Marlborough Railway half yearly meetings. The period from 1874 to 1881 was a time of relative calm for the MR and the advent of the SMA was reported on 28th September 1875 in the following statement from the directors...

The first sod of the Swindon, Marlborough and Andover was turned in July last by the Rt. Hon. Lord Ernest Bruce, M.P. Your Directors deem this a fitting opportunity to record the satisfaction of the event and it is their hope that before many years are passed they may be able to congratulate the shareholders of the Marlborough Railway on an increased revenue on their own line in consequence, as well as improved means of communication for the towns and district through which the proposed railway will pass.

The account was also received in 1877 for the narrowing of the gauge three years earlier, and at the pleasantly modest level of £296.11.8d, considerably less than the £2,600 originally quoted by the GWR in 1874!

One exception to the relative quiet of the period came on 3rd July 1878, the Marlborough company bringing an action against the GWR under the 'The Regulation of Railways Act 1873'. In dispute were certain tolls alleged not to have been paid on goods traffic since the time of opening. The case for the MR was set out in detailed legal terms but admitted '.....Your applicants are unable at present to state accurately the gross tonnage.....' The reply of the GWR was presented 12 days later and not unexpectedly refuted the various arguments of the MR. It was left then to the Railway Commissioners to pass judgement. The principles involved, legal and otherwise, were hardly landmarks,it would seem and 'the verdict' published on 23rd July 1878 comprised just 26 words, compared with the 1500+ involved in the application. The judgement read as follows: *Upon hearing the Attorneys or Agents on both sides (and by consent) We Do Order that this application be dismissed each party paying their own costs.*

There appears to have been no souring of relations between the MR and GWR and there is no evidence of an appeal being sought. It could hardly have been worth it. The MR minute books only refer briefly to the matter two months later when, it was stated, an agreement had been reached with the GWR for the credit of tonnage at the rate of 1/- per ton on coal instead of on a milage basis as previously. (These amicable sentiments are all the more striking when contrasted with the attitude of the GWR to other lines, notable the Didcot, Newbury & Southampton company.)

As can be seen from the traffic and dividend returns, receipts showed a respectable increase throughout the period - see Appendices 1 & 2. The figures announced on 19th September 1881 quoted £141.2.2d from the GWR for three telegraph wires, previously installed in February 1870.

Returning again to the fortunes - or otherwise, of the SMA, the directors of that company obviously regarded the completion of the connection between their line and that of the MR at Marlborough as vital to their survival. The first step was the signing of an agreement on 11th December 1881, between the MR, GWR and SMA as to the actual connection between the two railways at Marlborough. Apart from the requisite earthworks, the trackwork and signalling for the junction was to be

---

*. *There is some doubt as the the actual ruling gradient of the MR, various sources quote 1 in 58 to 1 in 75.*

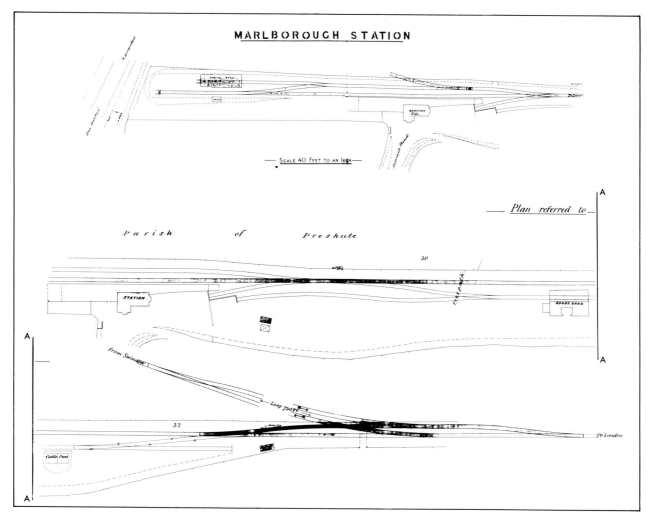

MARLBOROUGH STATION

Scale 40 Feet to an Inch

Plan referred to

Parish of Preshute

undertaken by the GWR, the SMA to pay £523 for this. The ground work began shortly afterwards and the new connection was ready for inspection by the Board of Trade on 21st March 1882, slightly less than eight months after the opening of the route from Swindon.

To haul the inspection train the SMA company provided their engine No. 4, more usually referred to as 'The Fairlie', or 'Jumbo' and known to have been the first in the country to be fitted with Walschaerts valve gear. In charge of the inspection was Major Marindin of the Board of Trade. The train was made up of two composite coaches, a guards van and four or five goods vans containing stores. The special started from Swindon and stopped first to inspect the new junction at Marlborough. At the same time a pilot engine was attached for that part of the journey over the MR. Following this the party proceeded to Savernake where some delay occurred as the junction points were spiked, after which the train continued south from Wolfhall Junction, east of Savernake, to Andover.

Major Marindin prepared his report shortly afterwards and was somewhat scathing at the way in which time had apparently stood still at Savernake.....

.....at Savernake Station on the Berks and Hants Railway which is used and worked by the Great Western Railway, the arrangements are such as would not be sanctioned upon a new line at the present time and are in many respects faulty. The junction of the Marlborough line with the Berks & Hants is not properly laid or signalled - there is a want of interlocking of the points and signals and there is only one platform at the station which is used as a passing place so that loaded passenger trains have to be backed from the platform into a loop.

I have therefore to report that although the fulfilment of the few requirements which I have noted as being necessary upon the new line and which have been ordered to be at once attended to, would render these lines,

including the junctions at Marlborough and at Wolfhall, in themselves satisfactory, and safe for the passenger traffic, yet in that inasmuch as no station has been provided for the reception of traffic at the north.....and south end.....of the Railway.....except at Savernake, which is not fit for the existing traffic and still less for the additional traffic which would pass through it upon the opening of the new lines, I must report that by reason of the incompleteness of the works, these new lines cannot be opened for passenger traffic without danger to the public using the same.

In addition to the alterations which are necessary at Savernake Station, block working should be introduced upon the Marlborough line before the through trains from Swindon to Andover can be safely run upon it.

The MR itself had been worked under the principle of 'One Engine in Steam' since the time of opening, official records showing this to be superseded by 'Train Staff and Ticket' around the period 1882/3, no doubt in direct consequence of the above inspection.

Such a derogatory report was naturally a considerable disappointment to both the SMA and MR companies; the prospect of through services receded accordingly, and the hoped-for increase in receipts eluded both concerns for the present. Whilst there is certainly no evidence to prove the point, the attitude at Paddington was surely one of quiet satisfaction.

Commencing almost immediately then, a storm of correspondence passed between the SMA and MR, pondering the required improvements. The SMA was willing to undertake the necessary work, including the changes at Savernake but the MR now found itself enmeshed in delaying tactics by the Great Western, the latter insisting that the cost of all works should be passed to the SMA and not just those works directly affecting SMA traffic. Matters were finally resolved later in the year but not before an expensive legal battle involving all three companies and the Railway Commissioners. The works at Savernake

(1533)

GREAT WESTERN RAILWAY

Return shewing cause of delay to DOWN PASSENGER TRAINS at Savernake & Box Station.

on Fri day, the 2nd of May 1884

The Station Master must personally supervise the preparation of this return, sign it himself, and see that every train is entered which may be booked to start from or call at his Station which is delayed over time; and also any train which may be checked or stopped out of course at his Signals or Station, giving the fullest explanation of all delays, and he must forward the return to the Divisional Superintendent as directed in Mr. Tyrrell's Circular No. 558, dated 21st April, 1884.

	Train from starting point		Booked time at this Station.		Actual time at this Station.		Delays at Signals.	Overtime at this Station.	Delays Waiting Connecting Trains.	Explanation of delay to be given here as per instructions above.
Time.	From	Arr.	Dep.	Arr.	Dep.				
6.10	Andover	7.7	7.8	7.7	7.10		2		Engine taking water
8.40	Savernake		8.40		8.42	Nil	Nil	2min	Waiting up
9.20	Andover	10.1	10.5	10.1	10.11		6	5	Waiting up
1.25	Savernake		1.25		1.28	Nil	Nil		Waiting up
10.58	do		10.58		11.4				
2/10 pm	Reading	3.42	3.44	3.43	3.46		1		
4.35	Savernake		4.35		4.38			3	left train 5 mins late
6/7	do		6.07		6.45		6	22	Down train 22 mins late,
6.25	Paddington	8.05	8.50	8.43	9.13	taken 4/			
9.17	Savernake		9.17		9.45			22	

Station Master.   [See back for UP PASSENGER TRAINS.]

---

and elsewhere were eventually completed and ready for use by the end of 1882 with the GWR, it is thought, undertaking much of it themselves. For reasons not completely clear there was no immediate reinspection of the line and not until 19th January 1883 did Col. Yolland attend the work:

.....I have inspected the alterations and additions which have been made by the GWR Co. at the Savernake Station on their own line and on that of the Marlborough Railway between Wolfhall and Marlborough Junction, with a view to the running of the through trains of the SM & AR Co. between Savernake (GW) and the Andover Junction Station. The works at Savernake Station have been constructed in accordance with the requirements of the Board of Trade as previously defined. Two new signal boxes have been provided, an East and a West signal box. The East Box contains a locking frame of 18 levers of which 4 are spare ones. The West Box contains a locking frame for 32 levers of which 5 are spare. The interlocking is correct. A second platform with shelter on it has been provided and an over footbridge for crossing from platform to platform. This is an exchange Station and a urinal should be put up on the new platform. Gauge ties are also required at the facing points. These items are to be provided at once. I understand the SM & A Co. have already given an undertaking that covers the working of their system between Swindon Junction and Andover Junction Station. This working is to be on the Train Staff and ticket system combined with the absolute block.....I have therefore to recommend that the Board of Trade do now sanction the opening of the line between Marlborough Junction and Grafton Stations for the passenger traffic of the SM & A Railway.

Other sources quote the date of inspection as 31st January 1883, but whichever is correct the way was now clear for the running of through services over the MR and these were duly instituted from 5th February 1883. (A shuttle service had operated between Andover and Grafton since 1st May 1882). Traffic on the MR increased considerably as a result of the through running now rendered possible; the MR directors were

able to report an extra 8,478 passengers and 1,938 tons of goods over their line in the period 5th February to 30th June 1883. They could thus recommend a dividend of 3%, the minimum figure for the remainder of the company's independent existence. Even so this increase in traffic is hardly as much as would perhaps be expected.

The SMA directors were acutely aware of the limitations of the section of line between Marlborough and Savernake especially as a considerable increase in traffic was envisaged when the neighbouring Swindon - Cheltenham Extension line was completed. The directors of the SMA and MR thus met on 1st November 1883 at the Westminster Palace Hotel, London, with the subject for discussion 'the proposed doubling of the Marlborough railway.' Evidently these talks met with agreement for the following day the SMA company secretary wrote officially with a proposal to double the MR from Marlborough Junction to a point a quarter of a mile north of Savernake station. The SMA line would then continue eastwards on an independent course parallel with the GWR before crossing the Berks and Hants to rejoin its own metals nearer Grafton. Cost of the second line of rails together with easing of the gradients was put at £75,000.

Accordingly the SMA applied to Parliament in 1884 for the necessary powers, the GWR in the meanwhile applying pressure to both parties against the scheme. This was enough and the Bill was withdrawn, on condition the GWR end their opposition to the SMA's associate company, the Swindon - Cheltenham which was then in the early stages of construction. Perhaps this was all the SMA had really hoped to achieve, for the SMA directors had long recognised their only hope for financial security lay in a complete north - south route.

It should be mentioned at this stage that the SMA were heavily burdened by the annual charges levied by the GWR;

£4,000 for the use of the MR and £1,000 for Savernake station. The SMA was now the M&SWJ* and these debts had been one reason for it falling into receivership. Quite understandably it was anxious to rid itself of the stranglehold of the GWR from Marlborough to Wolfhall Junction/Savernake and a nominally independent company was proposed in 1888, its purpose to build a new line between Marlborough and Grafton (the first station on the M&SWJ south of Savernake). The idea brought forth opposition from all quarters including the MR and GWR though probably there was little real likelihood of the scheme succeeding at this stage. For its part the MR conceded that if the proposal was dropped they would arrange for their own line to be doubled. How likely this might have been is unclear for the minutes of the MR do not mention the matter. Indeed the only reference concerns the MR, which would oppose the M&SWJ Bill and the appointment of a new chairman, Lord Henry Brudenell Bruce, M.P.

Clearly then the MR saw their own good fortunes threatened, for the extra M&SWJ traffic over the MR had resulted in dividends reaching no less than 4½% by the end of 1886, a not inconsiderable return on investment compared with other railway companies of the period. (By comparison the GWR reported a dividend of 2⅓% for the same period). Sadly, such good fortune was overshadowed by the death of the MR Chairman, Ernest Bruce. He was succeeded by Richard Edmonds Price from Bridgwater who had held the post of deputy chairman from about 1871.

One question emerges; had the MR directors realised that the time was approaching when an independent M&SWJ route was inevitable?

* P.26 The Midland & South Western Junction Railway by Colin Maggs, David & Charles 1967.

As would be expected the 1888 proposal for a Marlborough to Grafton railway fell into abeyance and for two reasons. One was the amount of effort already being expended by the M&SWJ in the completion of the Swindon - Cheltenham section of route and secondly, negotiations with the GWR had commenced over a new draft working agreement. T.B.Sands reports an interesting item from this proposed agreement, a passing place to be constructed between Marlborough and Savernake, or if the M&SWJ was to be doubled between Swindon and Marlborough, the GWR would also double the MR. This new agreement however was never fully completed and therefore could not be implemented.

It would be tempting at this stage to dwell further on the fortunes of the M&SWJ and their plans for expansion but to do so would be to divorce the text from the main theme of this book. Suffice it to say that following an unsettled period the Swindon - Cheltenham line was finally opened to passenger traffic on 1st August 1891 - more than ten years after the original Act authorising its construction.

From the 1880s onwards there was increased traffic over the little Marlborough Railway and a corresponding increase in dividends to the shareholders. This was especially so from 1891 when there was a further increase in traffic following upon the opening of the Swindon - Cheltenham route. After this dividends reached no less than £5. per cent *per annum* on at least two occasions during the 1890s. But what could well have been an amicable and profitable working arrangement between the three interested parties, the GWR, MR and M&SWJ was turned to an ugly confrontation by the belligerent attitude of the former.

As an example the GWR insisted upon a time consuming ticket inspection for all M&SWJ passenger trains calling at Savernake whilst the inflexibility of the 'staff and ticket' method of single line working meant that often a train would arrive at

The north end of the tunnel under Savernake Forest, the main engineering feat of the Marlborough and Grafton line, opened on 26th June 1898. The tunnel was approached from either end through a chalk cutting 70ft deep; whilst in this view it has a double line of rails, this varied over the years. The keystone to the arch at the south end of the tunnel bore an inscription from 'Georgina, Marchioness of Ailesbury.'

National Railway Museum

either Savernake or Marlborough only to find the 'staff' at the other end of the section. It was rumoured such delays were compounded by the loyalties of the respective company staff although as T.B. Sands has quoted, *.....in fairness it must be said that the timekeeping of trains on the M&SWJ.....was so bad that there was no knowing when a train would turn up at the junction.....*

The steep gradients of the MR were also a severe test to M&SWJ through trains and whilst the financial penalties imposed by the GWR have already been referred to, one further item on this subject may not be out of place. T.B. Sands again quotes as to the attitude of the GWR at that time *.....The GWR even tried on one occasion to extract a fare from the General Manager of the M&SWJ when he was travelling on the footplate of one of his company's engines between Marlborough and Savernake*.....*

Despite the various M&SWJ trains, local services on the MR continued throughout the period much as before, with additional services now available between Marlborough and Savernake only to the benefit of the local populace. For some years to come both Marlborough and Savernake would retain a railway service far in excess of the local need; the latter today remains a diminutive rural hamlet.

Accordingly delays to M&SWJ traffic continued as before leading in 1893 to a protracted correspondence between the M&SWJ and MR companies. The tone of the letters indicate that the M&SWJ was aware that the difficulties were not of MR making and that they had considerable sympathy as to the position they found themselves in. Sam Fay, the M&SWJ General Manager then asked the MR directors to use their influence with the GWR for the benefit of both companies.

The outcome was that during 1893 the 'electric train staff' was installed between Savernake and Marlborough in replacement of the 'staff and ticket'. This meant that trains could follow each other in the same direction once the first had arrived safely at either end of the line. But by then it was already too late as in the summer of the following year, 1894, another proposal for a Marlborough - Grafton railway was made, this time a decision to go ahead being postponed by the M&SWJ rather than defeated elsewhere. Shortly afterwards on 29th September 1894 at the half yearly meeting of MR shareholders, a proposal was mooted to sell the branch to the GWR, the first time such a possibility was publicly discussed. Evidently the proposal was well received by the floor, as shortly afterwards an approach was made to the GWR which by the end of the year had offered £120 worth of GWR stock for £100 of the MR equivalent.

The GWR offer was reported at the next meeting in March 1896 and unanimously accepted, the GWR to take over immediate control until the independent company was finally extinguished by Parliament. A report of the meeting appeared in *The Marlborough Times* for 30th March 1895 at which it was stated that not all of the shareholders were completely happy with new GWR monopoly of traffic but generally felt they had done well.

This was destined to be the last meeting of the MR to be held in Marlborough; the two subsequent meetings were held at Paddington with the last on 21st October 1896. The MR was absorbed by the GWR under the terms of 'The Great Western Railway (Additional Powers) Act 1896' which became law on 1st July 1896.

Whilst this had been taking place the M&SWJ had progressed with their proposed Marlborough and Grafton Railway, supported by the War Office who saw it as an improvement to the direct line to both Tidworth and Southampton. Opposition was finally limited to that of the GWR and was insufficient to prevent passing of the Act on 7th August 1896. Construction began almost immediately and the 5½ mile line was opened to traffic on 26th June 1898 with the connection at Marlborough between the MSWJ and former MR closed the following day. At that instant the original Marlborough Railway reverted to an insignificant branch.

Were the MR resigned to an eventual sell out? Could this have even occurred to the M&SWJ? Probably the attitude of the GWR was the crucial factor, the MR directors being aware that an independent M&SWJ line was inevitable; they would eventually have to sell up or lose heavily. The question was really one of timing, and the MR worked this to perfection assuring the maximum reward to all those who had invested. A takeover by the M&SWJ, even if this could have been afforded was unlikely as the GWR could still invoke difficulties at Savernake. The only alternative would have been a separate M&SWJ, just north of Savernake, as proposed in the 1880s but with this option gone the Marlborough and Grafton line became the inevitable outcome. But it need not have been so and the antagonism of the GWR seems to have been wholly responsible. Financially Paddington would pay dearly, and for long years, for their intransigence.

* T.B. Sands quotes the incident in relation to the 'General Manager' of the M&SWJ although regretfully no date is given. This was likely to have been either J.F.R. Daniel who held the post between 1885 and 1892 or Sam Fay if subsequent to 1892.

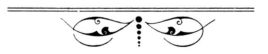

CHAPTER FIVE
SAVERNAKE STATION
and
THE BERKS & HANTS
MAIN LINE

Following a lavish and formal opening on 4th November 1862 the Berks and Hants Extension railway from Hungerford to Devizes opened to public traffic on 11th November. Four passenger stations were originally provided on the route, at Bedwyn, Savernake, Pewsey and Woodborough, each built by a Mr. W.H. Penning who was presumably a sub-contractor to Messrs. Smith and Knight, builders of the railway itself. Contemporary records suggest the cost of the stations amounted to £5,000 and this may be taken to refer to all four locations. The initial facilities were decidedly primitive and yet were perfectly adequate for what was in effect merely a single track meandering across country. The £5,000 also included a small

goods station at Burbage Wharf, just west of Savernake of which more will be discussed later.

There had been an amount of controversy over the precise siting of the stopping place at Savernake. Certain directors of the Berks and Hants Extension company together with Marlborough townsfolk felt that it should be built on the main road to Marlborough, close to the Kennet and Avon Canal and thus easily accessible for an interchange of traffic destined for Marlborough. (The fact that the distance between Burbage and Marlborough was still in excess of five miles and through Savernake Forest where the 'roads' were in effect no better than rutted cartways meant little; this was still a significant

The west end of Savernake station, with the main line towards London on the right and the Marlborough branch to the left. In the 'V' of the junction can be seen the West signal box, with a number of vehicles stabled on what was known as the 'transfer' and later the 'canal' siding. This had a capacity of only five four wheel vehicles and would probably be full with those shown (nearest the buffers is a siphon van, possibly used for milk). The limitations of this siding for goods transfer between the GWR and MSWJ are only too apparent. Notice the red signal arms for both the stop and distant signals - a change to yellow only began from 1927 onwards. Above the canal tunnel can be seen a wooden hut, which probably housed the engineering department trolleys. The light coloured wooden hut alongside the signal box was a linesman's cabin.

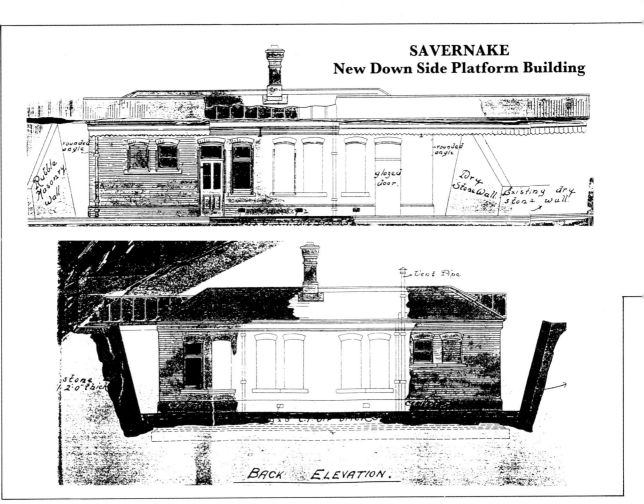

SAVERNAKE
New Down Side Platform Building

BACK ELEVATION.

Savernake station as rebuilt from 1898 onwards, in which form it survived for over 60 years. With the stopping place located in the parish of Burbage it is perhaps surprising that this name did not feature more significantly in the naming of the passenger station. Certain reports suggest that Burbage may well have been the suggested appellation and it was the major landowner in the area, the Marquess of Ailesbury, who was responsible for effecting the change. Other references make note of *Savernake Forest* station although it is not certain if this was ever displayed. The view is looking west towards Pewsey and clearly shows the covered footbridge and replacement buildings on the down side platform.

Lens of Sutton

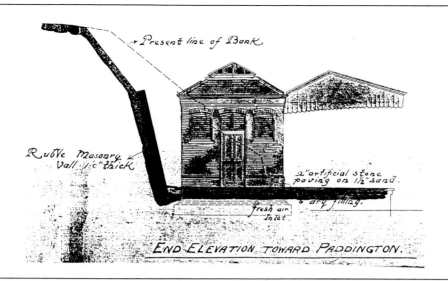

Present line of Bark

Ruble masonry
Vall 1'c" thick

2" artificial stone
paving on 1½" sand.

6 dry filling.

Fresh air
Inlet.

END ELEVATION TOWARD PADDINGTON.

The approach to the station, a sweeping driveway off the Burbage to Durley road. The drive slopes gently downhill to reach the level of the railway with the station located in a cutting. On the opposite side of the line can be seen the station master's house.

H.C.Casserley

improvement on the twelve miles from Marlborough to Swindon, and the previous nearest railway).

But a station near the main road was not at all popular with the engineer of the Berks and Hants Extension Railway , R.J. Ward, who strongly favoured a site above the canal tunnel at the foot of Durley Hill. This was the summit of the line, '.....and the only place suitable for a junction station, if a branch to Marlborough is ever to be built'.

With the Marlborough Railway having gained its Act of Parliament 18 months earlier, on 22nd July 1861 it is perhaps surprising to reflect upon the attitude of those individuals clamouring for the station to be built at an inappropriate point and Ward's comments were indeed based on fact - he was Engineer to the Marlborough Railway as well! After further discussion he was able to win the day and a passenger station was built in the location he advised; it was not envisaged that it would handle much in the way of goods traffic and instead a separate goods station was completed 68 chains - just over three-quarters of a mile - west of the new passenger station, at the nearest convenient point for interchange between the railway, the road to Marlborough and the Kennet and Avon Canal. This was christened Burbage Goods Station with the passenger station taking the name Savernake. (An interchange also existed near this point between the canal and road, named Burbage Wharf).

From contemporary reports it is possible to obtain a reasonably accurate picture of the working of the Berks and Hants line during these early days. Operated by the Great Western from the outset using that company's locomotives and rolling stock, it had been built to the broad gauge with just a single set of rails, although provision had been made in a number of the earthworks to accommodate a second track, should this later prove necessary.

As opened, Savernake station was of similar design to the stopping places at Bedwyn, Pewsey and Woodborough, a pleasing single storey mellow brick building with twin gables and the occasional lighter course of brick deliberately added to form a criss-cross pattern. Stone blocks at the corners and reproduction gothic arches completed an appearance intended to blend in with the lodge houses of the Marquess of Ailesbury which were located nearby. The station buildings rested within a cutting 30ft deep, which also marked the summit of the railway between Reading and Devizes.

Within the building the accommodation comprised the usual

booking and parcels offices together with 1st and 2nd class 'waiting and retiring' rooms and also a general waiting room and lobby; oddly enough no separate station master's office was indicated. The building stood on the up or London bound side of the line, for although Savernake was the only location with a loop (and as such the only passing place for trains between Hungerford and Devizes) no platform was then provided on the opposite, down, side. Passing loops were added at the other Berks & Hants Extension Railway stations from mid-1863 onwards, commencing with Pewsey.

In October 1863, a year after the opening of the station, a refreshment room was added alongside the main buildings. This was managed by a Mr. Maugham, the proprietor of the nearby *Savernake Forest Hotel* - itself built and opened around the same time. This privately owned hotel was constructed in similar style to the station and still survives today.

Access to the station was via a sloping driveway north of the railway which led off the Durley Hill road. This is the roadway seen in many of the photographs crossing the top of the station on the bridge. To connect Marlborough with the railway at Savernake a horse bus was provided. The service was operated by Mr. Hammond of the *Castle and Ball Hotel* in Marlborough who also operated the horse drawn bus service between Marlborough and Swindon, referred to earlier in this book. For some time the Savernake service was compelled to travel from Marlborough as far as Stibb Green in Burbage Village before turning back on itself to reach the station. This was due to the reluctance of the Marquess to allow the service to use the Savernake Forest estate roads. Not surprisingly then the bus became the subject of much criticism, only partly quelled by the opening of a new road from the Ram Alley turning, a saving in distance of about one mile.

It is not clear how long the bus survived although it may be reasonable to assume it ceased around the time of the opening of the railway to Marlborough in 1864. A motor operated bus service between the same locations was resurrected later by the GWR and this is discussed elsewhere.

The original train service on the Berks and Hants Extension befitted its role as a quiet cross country route with just four passenger trains each way on weekdays and two on Sundays. A number of these operated as mixed trains although from an unknown date a separate goods service was provided. These spartan arrangements were destined to last for over 20 years, surviving the gauge change - a far cry from the hectic summer service decades later.

Despite such leisurely provision Savernake saw a series of events which were to culminate in a potentially serious accident, on the single line to Pewsey. Highlighting the deficiencies in safety that existed on the railways around this time, the circumstances are briefly explained. On 2nd December 1862 a down passenger train arrived at Savernake bound for Devizes. It was then noticed that the driver of a previous goods train had been given the train staff as his authority to proceed rather than a ticket as should have been the case. To compound the difficulty no up train was due for over two hours to return this vital piece of equipment and there was also as yet no means of electric telegraph communication with Devizes.

Unknown to the railwaymen at Savernake, the mistake had been revealed as soon as the goods train reached Devizes and the engine was quickly detached and sent with all haste back towards Savernake - a perfectly safe move as the train staff should have guaranteed the protection of the engine over the line. But at Savernake events were moving towards potential disaster; the crew of the passenger train, tiring of the wait were allowed by the Station Master to proceed.... By sheer good fortune some men were working on the line near to Pewsey and saw both the light engine and passenger train approaching each

other from opposite directions on the single line. Incredibly they were able to warn the drivers of both engines who stopped in time. No details of sanctions against those responsible are recorded.

Despite such near catastrophe no immediate steps were taken to improve the safety of working and it was not until June 1864 that a set of draft proposals for working the line between Hungerford and Devizes with the assistance of the telegraph were prepared. Even so it was 1868 before the disc block telegraph was installed on the line. Around the same time additional passing loops were installed at Bedwyn, Pewsey and Woodborough but to discuss these changes further is to wander beyond the set bounds of this book and it is necessary to return again to Savernake and this time 1864, the year of opening of the branch line to Marlborough.

It is a matter of some regret that no track plan of Savernake, showing the actual layout in broad gauge days, appears to have survived although from the 1864 Board of Trade report covering the inspection of the Marlborough branch at the time of its opening - see Chapter 3 - a separate bay platform is referred to. This was located west of the Durley Hill road overbridge and on the north side of the main line. Official GWR records refer to expenditure of £29 10s 5d incurred in September 1863 related to 'moving signals,' possibly this was in anticipation of the Marlborough branch opening.

It would appear little in the way of change then affected Savernake station from 1864 until the time the gauge was changed from broad to narrow ten years later in 1874. Following conversion of the Wilts, Somerset and Weymouth lines from Weymouth through Frome to Thingley Junction (near Chippenham) the next railway to be dealt with was that from Southcote Junction (Reading) to Devizes and Holt. This took place on the night of 26th/27th June 1874 with the passage of a broad gauge engine the last movement prior to the engineers commencing work, all rolling stock having been removed previously. East of Hungerford the existing double line of rails allowed for a restricted train service although this was not the case through Savernake and instead it was not until the morning of 1st July that the service was resumed, both on the Berks and Hants Extension Railway and Marlborough Branch' with narrow gauge stock.

Again the lack of available track plans for the period restrict the amount of information available although it is believed the layout at Savernake was not altered at this time and still consisted of a single line with passing loop. It is not clear if any sidings existed for goods or carriage traffic but this is thought unlikely in the earliest days in view of a complaint from the Marquess of Ailesbury that the lack of suitable siding accommodation at the station meant he had sometimes to send his horses to Hungerford for loading. By 1877 a single short siding is shown trailing into the up line at the east end of the platform. This would appear to have formed a loading dock. The Marlborough branch junction consisted of a single lead trailing into the main line at a point just west of the end of the main line loop with the branch bay platform only accessible to trains from Marlborough. This restricted layout would have meant that the branch engine was forced to run around its train on the main line prior to returning to Marlborough. Quite naturally, such an arrangement was far from ideal both for the branch and main line services. For on the main line when loaded passenger trains were booked to cross at the station one of them had to back into the loop - a most undesirable practice with falling gradients at each end of the station and little or no interlocking between the points and signals.

Perhaps surprisingly the gauge conversion was not inspected immediately by the Board of Trade; instead it was three years later in 1877 that the first reference as to an appraisal of the

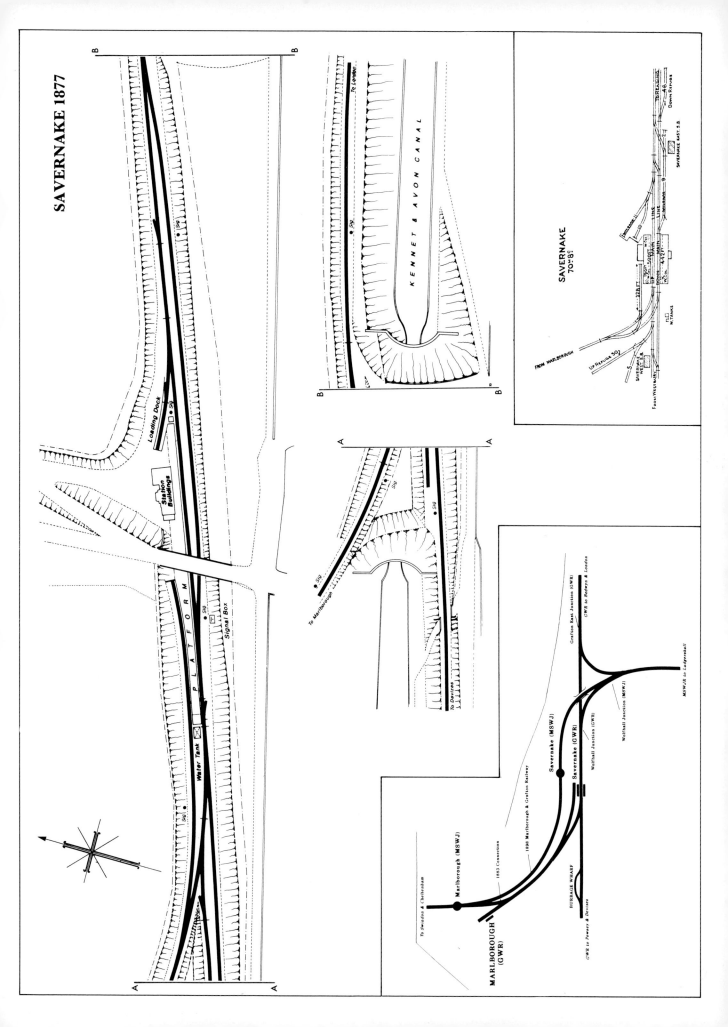

SAVERNAKE 1877

PLATFORM

Station Buildings

Loading Dock

Water Tank

Signal Box

Sig

Sig

Sig

Sig

Sig

Sig

B   B

A   A

To London

KENNET & AVON CANAL

Sig

To Marlborough

To Devizes

Sig

Sig

Sig

B   B

A   A

SAVERNAKE
70 M 8 C

FROM MARLBOROUGH

Up Refuge 50?

SAVERNAKE
WEST S.B.

From YESTBURY

DOWN MAIN LINE
UP MAIN LINE

W.C. W

W.TANKS

328 FT

BP 500FT W 6I

4 42 FT M

DETESINE

SAVERNAKE EAST. S.B.

46C

Down Refuges

MARLBOROUGH
(GWR)

To Swindon & Cheltenham

Marlborough (MSWJ)

1883 Connection

1898 Marlborough & Grafton Railway

Grafton East Junction (GWR)

GWR to Bedwyn & London

Savernake (MSWJ)

Savernake (GWR)

Wolfhall Junction (GWR)

Wolfhall Junction (MSWJ)

MSWJR to Ludgershall

BURBAGE WHARF

GWR to Pewsey & Devizes

revised works is found, the area covering Savernake and the Marlborough branch forming part of a complete inspection of the line from Hungerford to Holt Junction. The following extract relates to the local area:

I have the honour to report for the information of the Board of Trade.....that I have inspected the line of the Great Western Railway, from Hungerford to Holt Junction a distance of about 32 and a half miles, the gauge of which was altered from broad to narrow about June 1874. The whole of this line is single, with loop lines or sidings at the stations, and the alteration of the Gauge has been affected by shortening the transomes and pulling in the longitudinals on which the rails are laid.....From the length of time which has elapsed since.....(the line was).....opened for traffic, the replacing of large numbers of the original rails by new ones is urgently required, and is being done at the present time, to some extent the fencing is also in a bad state in many parts.....The Company have completed the interlocking of the Points and Signals at the following Stations..... - Burbage (Goods Station only) - 10 levers of which 2 are spare ones.....Savernake station has not yet been re-arranged. I saw a plan of what was intended to be done in respect of the re-arrangement of the lines, and I beg to mention that the junction with the Marlborough Branch, which is situated at the present west end of the Station, should form a complete double line junction with the Loop Lines of the Main Lines, Hungerford to Devizes.....Clocks are required at all the Stations .....the line between Hungerford and Devizes is worked with the assistance of the Electric Telegraph, without any Train Staff, under which system the passing places for trains are frequently changed, according to the exigences of the traffic. Under this system, several terrible collisions have taken place attended with great loss of life, and the Board of Trade determined about 2 years since, after the collision which occurred at Thorpe near Norwich on the Great Eastern Railway, not to sanction the opening of single lines for traffic unless the train staff system of working was combined with the absolute block system. The company have not yet completed their arrangements for doing this, nor have they as far as I know signified their intention of complying with this requirement. I have now therefore to report that, by reason of the incompleteness of the works, as specified in the present report, the opening of the line for Public Traffic from Hungerford to Holt Junction will be attended with dangers to the Public using the same and should not in consequence in my opinion, receive the sanction of the Board of Trade.

A copy of Colonel Yolland's report was forwarded to the GWR at Paddington and with the rider that *.....in the event of the Directors of the Great Western Railway disregarding the requirements contained in the report, the whole responsibility of any danger that may arise therefrom will rest with the Directors.*

Strong words indeed from a Board of Trade Inspector, and consequently a number of questions immediately arise. Firstly of course the line was already open for traffic and the comments in relation to the opening appear strange. Could it be then that the Board of Trade had no power to order the closure of a line already open - certainly this would seem to be the case. In addition, there is no mention of a re-inspection of the Marlborough branch itself or for that matter any comment on its own method of working. It might also be asked if the previous 'near miss' a few years earlier had been taken into consideration in recommending this change in working.

Despite the apparent urgency of Col. Yolland's report it was not until six weeks later, on 23rd June 1877 that the GWR replied to the Board of Trade report. Certain items are of particular interest not the least the apathy of the railway company when faced with criticism. Certainly this is the impression gained from contemporary reports although it may well have been that, privately, *heads did roll*. Certainly in following years improvements were made although it was to be some time yet before the GWR was accorded the mantle of safety by the same Board of Trade. The railway's freedom from serious accidents around this time was a matter in which luck certainly contributed a great deal.

.....I am desired in reply thereto to state, that the Directors regret that the Board of Trade should think it necessary in such a communication to remind them that the responsibility rests upon them for the working of the line, a matter on which they desire me to say they have never had any doubts.

With regard to the remarks contained in Colonel Yolland's report, I am to make the following observations:

The Engineer reported to the Board that in his opinion, new rails are not urgently required, as although some have been in use for some years, the road is in a perfectly safe condition.....Savernake Station has not yet been re-arranged, as a line called the Swindon and Andover Railway, which has been authorised, will if made form a junction at this point, and if the station were re-arranged now, it would probably have to be altered when the new line in question is constructed, for which reason it was considered advisable to defer carrying out the alterations, until it was seen where the new line would actually join ours. No progress however has been made with the works of this line and unless there is some assurance of its being made within a reasonable period the station will be re-arranged.

The report continued, *.....With respect to the remarks of Colonel Yolland as the mode of working the line between Hungerford and Devizes.....I am to remind the Board of Trade, that the line in question.....was originally worked with the Train Staff system, and that in consequence of complaints made by the public of the inconvenience caused by such mode of working, the Department upon the representations then made to them by the Directors of the Berks and Hants Extension Railway, and upon the report of Colonel Yolland himself, especially sanctioned the mode in which the Traffic upon the line has been with perfect safety worked since 1864.....*

The letter was signed by James Grierson, the GWR's General Manager.

At this point it may also be of interest to refer briefly to the fortunes of the Swindon, Marlborough and Andover Company at the time of the GWR's letter - 23rd June 1877. Work on the new line had actually commenced in July 1875 but ceased little more than a year later in October 1876 with funds exhausted. The GWR had opposed the new route almost from its inception and, it would seem in 1877, had not altogether given up hopes for its complete demise - see bibliography for further reading on the subject. This would go some way perhaps to explaining the reticence of the GWR as regards its intentions at Savernake although with the land terriers for the SMA sanctioned by Parliament consequent upon the passing of its Act in 1873 it is perhaps a little surprising that improvements had not been made to Savernake, which would allow for the future extension.

Construction work on the Swindon Marlborough and Andover resumed at an undisclosed date in late 1879 although before this, on 22nd March 1879 the GWR had eventually submitted plans to the Board of Trade for a rebuilding of Savernake station.

.....as no progress has been made with the work (referring to the proposed Swindon and Andover line) *and there appears to be no prospect of the line being made for some little time it has been decided to go on with the work of re-arranging and locking the Savernake Station. But before proceeding with the work I beg to submit the enclosed plan, showing what is proposed to be done and I shall be glad to hear that it meets with the approval of the Board of Trade.*

The letter was again signed by Grierson.

The practice of submitting plans in advance of work being carried out was certainly not unique though the earlier comments of Colonel Yolland probably had some bearing on the matter. The new layout would still not appear to include a double junction for the branch, as had been suggested two years earlier.

There is no evidence that whole or even part of the revised layout was in fact ever completed at Savernake; in March 1882 Major Marandin of the Board of Trade paid a visit in connection with his inspection of the completed SMA route and

From the station approach. The two sidings forming the small goods yard are visible; they were unusual in that a catch point was built into the turnout where they converged, prior to joining the main line. That to the left was known as the 'mileage' siding and could accommodate ll four wheel vehicles; the right hand siding was able to store 10 four wheel vehicles. At an unknown date a proposal was made to close the goods yard at Burbage Wharf and concentrate all facilities at Savernake, estimated to cost £1,500, though this was never carried out. The limited goods yard accommodation at the station had long been the subject of criticism particularly from the Marquess of Ailesbury but official GWR Minutes (undated) report the cost of an additional siding at the station to have been £350. The door visible in the main station building fronted a small lobby, which led into the booking office. Over the years a number of the rooms within the station changed their use according to differing traffic patterns, including the room to the left of the entrance door. Originally the second class waiting room, it was later the porter's office.

Lens of Sutton

Savernake station in 1965. Throughout its life no mains electricity was available and instead the buildings were illuminated by gas. The concrete lamp posts were erected in the 1930s from which pressurised paraffin lamps were hung when required. In the early years of the present century the GWR evolved a method of identifying each location within its empire by means of a number, which was then used in the despatch of traffic as well as internal mail. In January 1911 the following were allocated to the Savernake area: *Grafton Curve Box 530; Wolfhall Junction Box 531; Savernake East Box 532; West Box 534; Savernake Station 533; Burbage Box 535; Marlborough 665; Marlborough Engine Shed 666.* **It is not certain how long these remained in use but today the Western Region utilise a similar system for their office correspondence, unified under the term 'C.P.'- Collection Point - followed by an individual number.**

P.J.Kelley

was somewhat scathing as to the basic facilities then existing. The subsequent history of Savernake station is very much interwoven with the fortunes of the SMA line from this time on. A glance at the accompanying plan will enable the reader to identify the various locations referred to, the new SMA line diverging south from the main route at Wolfhall Juction en route to Andover.

The intransigence of the GWR with regard to an upgrading at Savernake is but another example of how that company responded to events in the nineteenth century and the venomous and continued campaign waged against the SMA was certainly not unique; nor was it unknown elsewhere in the country. Placed in the middle of these events was the independent Marlborough company which appears to have made no comment one way or the other. No doubt a very wise decision.

Although it is not always possible to identify exactly when changes at Savernake did occur, changes there certainly were and it would appear fairly certain that these were put into effect very rapidly after the official inspection of March 1882, the Board of Trade having insisted on alterations prior to SMA trains using Savernake station.

This work involved the provision of a second platform on the down side 300ft x 12ft upon which stood a small wooden waiting shelter. At the same time the track layout was altered, the passing loop on the main line extended and a double junction provided onto the Marlborough branch. A single compound was used to afford access to and from the bay platform onto the new double line. The double track branch resumed its single line course after a short distance and to cater for the interchange of vehicles between the SMA and GWR a transfer siding was provided at the west end of the station between the canal bank and Marlborough branch. This arrangement lasted until transfer sidings were completed at Wolfhall Junction.

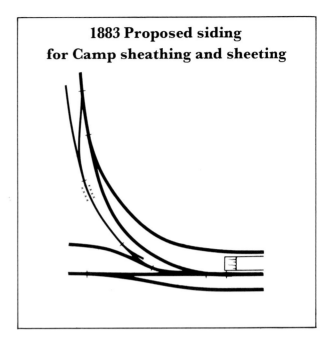

1883 Proposed siding for Camp sheathing and sheeting

On 9th November 1882 the GWR informed the SMA that the cost of these changes would be £4,660 and the work completed by 25th December 1882. It may be assumed that interlocking between points and signals also now existed whilst to accompany the changes to the track layout a number of signal alterations had also been necessary (See diagram). Around this time block telegraph working was installed on the Marlborough branch, intended to ease operation of the

The station from the west end with the nameboard proclaiming 'SAVERNAKE JUNCTION FOR MARLBOROUGH'. As can be seen, this wording was spaced on two separate boards and may have given rise to some confusion in the naming of the station over the years. The purpose of the boarded-in archway is not reported. In later years, possibly in the war period 1939/45, an additional brick building was erected on the down platform, between the overbridge and footbridge. Its function is not clear but may well have been used for parcels, or as a cycle store. The arch formed above the bay platform was useful as a covered area for the platform trolleys.

Looking east from the end of the platform, with the small goods yard visible to the left. On the right is the down goods loop, referred to as a mileage siding in certain official records. Savernake East signal box lies beyond in the background. The goods loop was of limited value to down trains due to a limited capacity of nine wagons and instead trains would sometimes set back into a refuge siding just east of the signal box, which could accommodate 46 vehicles.

Lens of Sutton

additional SMA traffic. The cost of the block telegraph was reported as £247 12s 4d and which was charged to the SMA.

It is not certain if a footbridge was provided at this time. Certainly the example which later existed at the station bore the date 1883 although early plans show one slightly west of this position, physically attached to the side of the road over-bridge. What is clear is that the footbridge which appears in early photographs was originally open to the elements and a covering in standard GWR style was only added some years later.

In the changes and improvements wrought at Savernake the GWR had already scored success over the SMA for, as might be recalled from Chapter 4, Major Marindin had recently criticised the GWR over the lack of facilities at the station. With the advent of the SMA the GWR found a convenient method of securing the necessary improvements at no cost to themselves. A bitter pill to the already financially shaky SMA which at the time had no other option open. All the harder to bear, doubtless, was the need not only to finance the necessary additional facilities for their own trains but changes which the GWR should by rights have already carried out themselves, over previous years. Neither was this sharp practice unusual in the GWR's history - just a few miles east, the 1908 rebuilding of Newbury was almost entirely at the expense of the Didcot, Newbury & Southampton Company. (See *The Didcot, Newbury & Southampton Railway*, Wild Swan.). As far as the SMA was concerned such chicanery would not be forgotten and would later add weight to the need for an independent route from Marlborough, bypassing Savernake GWR altogether.

The following year, 1883, saw the erection of new signal boxes at the east and west ends of the station, described in detail later in the chapter.

A GWR document dated 10th May 1883 suggests some additional sidings may have been added alongside the branch around the same time. The location of the first of these is shown on the accompanying plan, for 'Camp sheathing and sheeting'.

No explanation as to this term is given although it does tend to imply a military purpose. The same document refers to an additional siding to be added, alongside the up main line and opposite the new East signal box. This time no plan is given. There is no evidence to prove either of these were ever actually laid.

The station now settled down to a relative calm, a period which continued for some 15 years until 1898. The first event of significance came on 26th June 1898 and involved the opening of the Marlborough and Grafton line connecting the two sections of the former SMA route north and south of Savernake. In so far as the GWR station at Savernake was concerned there was now competition from a new Savernake station serving the M&G route and located a short distance north of the Berks and Hants Extension line. Both the M&G line as well as the connections at Wolfhall Junction are discussed in detail elsewhere in the narrative.

More important was the GWR decision to incorporate the majority of the Berks and Hants lines in the new shortened route to the west, which involved doubling of the main line throughout as well as a general easing of curves and in places gradients. Beyond Patney and Chirton station a new line was to be built running west along the Stert valley to Westbury. To permit of the doubling of the original line, whilst continuing to operate a regular service on the route, a number of temporary installations were made at various locations on the Berks and Hants lines. Again it would be tempting to diverge into details concerning this work although to do so would be to take the narrative away from the theme of the text; suffice to say that the Board of Trade were informed whenever a temporary connection was made which affected a passenger carrying line.

As far as the local area was concerned, the new works were brought into use in stages, and although it was originally hoped to have it finished by the end of 1898, the double line east of Wolfhall Junction was not opened for traffic until 8th January

A branch train at Savernake, in the down main platform. The photograph was taken in 1928 and shows a Metro tank at the head of the two former MSWJ bogie vehicles, by this time repainted in the standard GWR chocolate and cream livery. A number of MSWJ vehicles were retained by the GWR after the former company was absorbed, with a two coach rake finding regular employment on the Marlborough - Savernake shuttle. The reasons for the branch train standing in the main platform are not explained. On the platform however can be seen the lamp hut (another was located at the east of the station) whilst the station water tanks are visible at the top of the cutting.
Lens of Sutton

Still in GWR livery some years after nationalisation, 2-6-2T No. 5510 on the branch at Savernake, having apparently just reversed out of the bay platform. In the background the route of the line through the High Level station, closed to all traffic in 1959, can be followed - the field beyond the engine was to have been the original site for the station master's house and at one time was in the ownership of a Mr. Read. In 1901 the GWR agreed to supply water to a cattle trough in this field.
E. Gamblin

A 'Castle' passing Savernake West box on the 8.20 a.m. Penzance-Paddington. The boarding under the box windows has been removed, revealing the brickwork beneath - the lower courses having weathered over the years. In the right background it is possible to discern the Marlborough branch, converging into a single set of rails. The up refuge, which could accommodate 50 4-wheeled vehicles, is also just visible, by the fence.
B.Y. Williams

1899. This was followed on 15th October 1899 by the section from Savernake west through Burbage and finally on 19th November 1899 the short missing piece between Savernake East and Wolfhall Junction. The delay on this last section was attributed to '.....difficulties relating to the construction of certain bridges for an adjoining landowner'. Messrs. Pauling & Co., Contractors, were responsible for the work.

Board of Trade records show that an inspection occurred on 7th January 1899. On this date Colonel Yorke visited the route between Hungerford and Wolfhall Junction and apart from recommending a speed restriction until the new works had consolidated, had no adverse comments to make, a situation somewhat different from that of a few years earlier. (A 20 mph limit over the new works was confirmed by the GWR three days later). The Colonel did pass favourable comment as to the track ....laid with steel rails weighing 92 lbs. per yard and cast iron chairs weighing 46 lbs. each. The sleepers are 9 ft. x 10 ins. x 5 ins. and are laid at varying distances, the maximum being 2 ft. 11 ins. from centre to centre. Official records fail to give a date when the longitudinal baulks had been replaced. (The double track between Wolfhall Junction and Savernake together with the section west to Patney and Chirton was inspected on 1st November 1901).

The turn of the century was witness to a change in the type of traffic seen at the station, for with the opening of the M&SWJ's Marlborough and Grafton railway in 1898, gone were that company's trains; instead the Marlborough branch had returned to the type of existence it had enjoyed from 1864 to 1883. On 26th June 1898 the connection at Wolfhall Junction between the GWR main line and the M&SWJ was closed although Wolfhall Junction signal box remained 'open' until sometime in 1899. It is not clear if the trackwork between the two systems was left in situ or removed. From 1st November 1900 a slight softening of attitudes appears to have taken place for the connection was re-instated for use of transfer traffic and then for through traffic from 28th July 1902.

The year 1900 had also seen the opening of the Stert and Westbury railway with express trains for Weymouth now able to take advantage of the new route. It was not until 1906 that the final section of cut-off from Castle Cary to Langport was ready for traffic and this led to West of England trains using the line through Savernake.

Whilst this work had been going on Savernake station had also been extended. Official records show that on 30th November 1898 approval was given for £3,796 to be spent on the following items:

Extension of up and down platforms to 500 ft.
Additional waiting room and lavatory on down side
Footbridge to be covered and new veranda on down side
New goods lock up for down side
New loading bank
Additional siding and crossover (these were located at the east end of the station and with the new siding parallel with the original single siding whilst the crossover formed a trailing connection on the main line nearby).
Slewing of down refuge siding and new up refuge siding.

For reasons that are not explained it would appear the work took some time to complete and it may have been as late as 1903 before all was finally ready. This assumption is based on the accompanying official notice of that date. An entry in the official Engineering Department records reveals that excess expenditure of £1,194 was incurred on the work.

Photographs reveal the extent of the changes and clearly show the replacement down side buildings and altered footbridge, the cutting side having been excavated to accommodate the new down side buildings. The platform extension was at the east end of the station.

TRAFFIC HANDLED

Despite its importance as a junction and later interchange between the GWR and M&SWJ, traffic using Savernake was limited throughout the life of the station. That is, of course, not to say that few passengers or freight vehicles were seen at the station but rather traffic *originating* from the location was limited. The reasons for this are simply explained - the area around the station was primarily rural and as such there were few passengers to be lured.

In addition the relatively empty countryside was well served by railways. So much so that at its peak there were no less than eight other stations and yards within a 5¼ mile radius of Savernake, including the GWR station itself. Principal amongst these in relation to local traffic were the neighbouring MSWJ Savernake station and the same company's Grafton and Burbage stopping place. Indeed the latter appears to have attracted much of the local traffic from Burbage village at the expense of the GWR. Savernake Great Western was left then to collect what remained - in practice precious little.

A glance at the traffic statistics for the station reveals these shortcomings in detail. As far as Savernake GWR is concerned it can be seen from the figures that the number of tickets issued peaked at 19,544 as early as 1913. The figure then fell steadily until by 1938 it had reached 6,928. (The 1938 statistics refer only to the period January - November. It is unlikely that the last month of that year would have shown a significant increase). Season tickets showed a similar decline, much of it attributable to increased road competition, then beginning to secure a foothold in the rural areas. A further factor was the general recession of the economy for the period.

On the freight side it is known that there was no local coal merchant based at Savernake station and instead a number of local firms had fuel delivered to the station whenever it was their intention to deliver round about. Although unconfirmed it may well have been that a large quantity of the coal received each year was destined for Tottenham House. Another possibility is that at one time fuel for Crofton pumping station on the Kennet and Avon canal was also dealt with locally.

As might be expected, most of the goods traffic originating from the station was agricultural and included sugar beet, fertilizers and animal feedstuffs. Again though this was limited and there was also competition from the nearby Burbage Wharf goods station. Indeed it must be said that it appears strange the latter location survived as long as it did. Parcels and livestock were also dealt with including race horses from a number of local stables.

One produce poorly documented is milk. Certainly it is known that at one time the rival M&SWJ station at Savernake boasted facilities for handling it, from a Wiltshire Farmers' Co-operative and as such it is reasonable to assume milk was also dealt with at the GWR station. It is unfortunate then that milk traffic is not referred to under a separate heading in the official traffic statistics. Evidence comes from the working timetable for July 1915 in which there is reference to an evening passenger and milk train leaving Marlborough at 6.33 p.m. and arriving at Savernake at 6.45 p.m. The churns were then transferred to an up milk service which left Savernake at 8.10 pm. This left a return passenger working from Savernake to the branch terminus at 8.03 pm. arriving at 8.15 pm. (Both the Sunday milk service and return passenger working varied over the years. Some timetables show the service as an engine and van from Savernake to Marlborough returning with the milk traffic. The various workings are discussed in more detail in the chapter on the working of the line).

No reference has been found to the GWR employing a local

carrier at the station although from about 1929 the area was covered by the railway operated road motor lorries under the zonal arrangement. No road vehicle was based at Savernake or Marlborough and instead the nearest vehicles were at Bedwyn, Devizes and Swindon.

STAFF

Wrongly dated. My dad Bill Scott was in the Royal Navy unt.l 1945

References to the staff at Savernake are incomplete and in order to gain an approximate picture of those employed at the station it is necessary to make recourse to a variety of sources, certain of which appear to conflict slightly, especially with regard to initials and also starting and finishing dates. The following is as accurate a picture as possible in the circumstances.

There was a Station Master in charge at Savernake from an early date, probably from the time the station opened. The first reference to this incumbent appears in December 1862 when Mr. Coombs was suspended for allowing the westbound train to proceed onto the single line without the authority of the train staff. His subsequent fate is not recorded.

There is now no record of the name of the Station Master until 1899 at which time Arthur Edward Murphy was in charge. By 1903 George Wilmot is recorded in the post although he was succeeded in November 1906 by Mr. S.C. (Charles) Clements who was promoted from his previous position of booking clerk at Didcot. By 1911 Francis Brown was in charge and then in March 1914 G.(?) W. Barnby arrived from Wooburn Green. Mr. Barnby left in April 1919 to take up a similar post at Codford on the Westbury to Salisbury line and was succeeded at Savernake almost immediately by William Henry Upton, from Witham. Mr. Upton stayed until December 1934 when he moved to Melksham and the following month, January 1935, Mr. F.T. Fawden was appointed having

Savernake and area staff, 1942. Left to right - 'Artie' Stroud, porter; Dick Davis, shunter; Peggy Ruddle, signalwoman at Grafton; Ron Millard, Station Master; Olive Brettelle, clerk; Bill Scott, porter and Thelma Hoara, signalwoman at Collingbourne.

Collection Adrian Vaughan

held the same position at Wishford. It is not certain how long Mr. Fawden remained at Savernake and by 1942 Ron Millard was in charge. The final entry during Great Western days appears in November 1946 when Mr. W.A.F. Oram came to Savernake as Station Master from his previous employment of goods clerk at Devizes; he remained in charge until 1958 when the position was abolished at the station.

At this stage it should be mentioned that the Great Western system of grading station masters was based on a scale of 1-6, the lowest number being the highest grade. There were in addition certain special grades to cover the largest stations. The clerical grades adopted a similar role and so a station might possess a Class 3 Station Master whilst the clerk would always be at least one grade below, viz. Grade 4. Promotion for clerks was therefore either to a higher grade within their own department or to the Station Master grade. Signal staff could also apply for transfer to a similar post although in all cases this was dependent upon successfully passing the qualifying examinations in station accountancy.

Station gradings were known to alter over the years to correspond with changing traffic patterns but it is not known if Savernake had always enjoyed Class 3 status.

Housing was provided for the Station Master at Savernake from at least 1912, though the first references appear some years earlier, on 20th July 1898 in correspondence emanating from the Divisional Engineers office at Paddington. In this it is suggested the ideal siting would be to the north of the main line

Doreen Spackman, Station Master Ron Millard and Olive Brettelle at Savernake in 1942. The ladies were employed by the railway in place of men serving with the armed forces.

Collection Adrian Vaughan

Savernake West signal box, which dated from 1883. The structure is shown in almost original condition and retains its timber boarding beneath the windows - this was removed at a later time. The box measured 22ft 2ins x 7ft to the operating floor and contained a 32 lever frame. This is thought to have been of a very old type with a mixture of double and 'single twist inlocking.' Official records show that cast iron nameplates were ordered for the two Savernake boxes from Reading Signal Works on 28th February 1899.

H.M.R.S.

above the Marlborough bay platform. The question was also asked by the engineering department as to whether the existing water supply to the station might be suitable for use as drinking water - possibly with the aid of filtration equipment as this would then avoid the need for what would probably be a 120ft deep well.

In the event a site south of the main line and almost opposite the Savernake Forest Hotel was selected where a well of 88 ft. 7 ins. depth was sunk. A sample of water from this taken in June 1911 was declared unsafe for drinking. The well was then pumped out several times and a further sample analysed the following month; this was cleared for drinking - even if the Swindon Chemist's report revealed its colour to be a 'Light brownish grey tint.' At the same time a sample taken from the station water tank revealed its contents to be totally unfit for drinking. Minutes state that approval for the station master's house, whatever the shortcomings of the water, was given on 15th December 1910 at an estimated cost of £441. The contract was let to J. Edwards & Sons and with the actual cost (January 1912) reported at £450 10s 5d.

Aside from the station master, the station boasted the usual complement of clerks, signalmen, porters, shunters, etc. and by 1911 had a thriving ambulance class combined with its neighbour at Marlborough. No other living accommodation was built for other grades of employee.

The station master was in overall charge of the signalmen in the area which included Burbage Wharf, Savernake West and East, Wolfhall Junction, Grafton East Junction and the level crossing at Crofton on the main line east towards Bedwyn. The number of signalmen varied over the years according to the hours the boxes were open as well as the working hours per week. At Savernake itself there had been a grade of 'signal-porter' which as the name implies involved varied duties according to traffic requirements. Conditions however were hard and the pay poor. In 1914 a signal porter might expect '20 shillings, rising to 21 shillings, for a 66 hour week with 1 hour

Alongside the Marlborough bay platform in 1942, left to right - Herbert Bint, guard; Len Chick, driver; Percy King, fireman; Sid New, shunter; and 'Artie' Stroud, porter.

Collection Adrian Vaughan

daily for meals. After one year, three days leave was granted, rising to six days after fifteen years service'. As a comparison at the same time a Class 2 porter (porter grades should not be compared with the clerical grades) received 18/- weekly. Conditions were still harsh in 1924 for on 5th March an application was made by the Savernake porters for their Sunday duties to be restricted to 12 hours. This was agreed by the GWR.

By 1934 official records give a more accurate assessment of the station staff as follows:

Station Master Class 3
1 Booking Clerk, junior
2 Porters, class 2
2 Goods Shunters
Signalmen: Wolfhall Junction, 1 Class 4
 Savernake East, 3 Class 4
 Savernake West, 2 Class 4
1 Crossing Keeper, Crofton Crossing
1 Porter/Shunter at Burbage

At this time supervision was also exercised over the two remaining staff at Savernake High Level Station.

A 1938 report makes a slight amendment in that the Burbage post is that of Porter/Signalman whilst only one man is now employed at Savernake High Level. No details are given as to the number of signalmen in the area.

Finally in 1946 it was reported that the Junior Clerk had been replaced by three female clerks whilst there were also three porters at the station. All other posts were as in 1938 and again there is no mention of the signalmen - presumably they were referred to in a separate register. The additional clerks and porter for the 1946 period are simply explained through additional wartime traffic. Moves however were afoot in late 1946 to reduce staff numbers to a figure more in keeping with the traffic handled.

The GWR staff magazine besides providing a fairly comprehensive month by month account of staff movements throughout the system also affords an insight into certain other staff affairs. One of these comes in November 1928 when the Savernake Lineman, A. Tillan, and his assistant, F. Hailstone were 'commended' though curiously no reference is made as to the circumstances which brought this about. In March 1936 the magazine contains a reference to the retirement of Mr. George New, a signalman at Savernake who had completed 43 years service, 35 of which were spent at Savernake. He was presented with an arm chair, letter rack and a brass bell by his colleagues.

Another employee having a long association with the station was Mr. A.L. Foster who, the *GWR Magazine* states, retired in May 1946 after 44 years and 11 months service at Wolfhall Junction signal box. The citation referred to the fact he had commenced at that location in 1901. This is at variance with official records as to the opening date of the new signal box at that location.

Savernake was also the meeting of two (Engineering Department) permanent way gangs: gang No. 49 with responsibilities from 67 miles 0 chains to 69 miles 40 chains included Grafton East Curve, and also gang No. 50 whose responsibility ran from 69 miles 40 chains to 72 miles 3 chains. It is known that gang No. 50 was also later responsible for part of the former M&SWJ line though whether in earlier times they had looked after the Marlborough branch is unclear.

Gang No. 49 were successful in winning the annual GWR Bristol Division prize for the best kept length of permanent way in 1935. Those concerned are recorded as Ganger E. Phillips, Sub-Ganger Fl. Lanfear and Lengthmen W. Wells, J. Andrews and J. Cox.

WATER SUPPLIES TO THE STATION

The subject of the water supplied to the station is of some significance, due to the close proximity at this point of the Kennet and Avon canal. This had opened in 1810 in direct competition with the stage coaches working between London and Bristol. The coming of the railway was an ill fortune for the canal and, as well chronicled elsewhere the Kennet and Avon was taken over by the GWR from 1st July 1851. Much of the correspondence relating to the waterway and water supply to the station carries the unexpected heading *GWR ENGINEERS OFFICE (CANALS) BATH.*.

The first item of significance is dated September 1877 and refers to the amount of water consumed at Savernake; other papers from October 1878 onwards refer to an alteration in the train timings on the Marlborough branch rendering it impossible for the branch engine to pump water at Savernake. This meant a light engine movement from Marlborough to Savernake and return, either before or at the termination of the day's service. Understandably, the suggestion was made that a small boiler be fitted in the pump house at Savernake, thus saving the expense. The pump house itself was located on the north side of the bay platform and was fitted with two steam pumps, which remained in use until at least November 1936. Approval was then given for an electrically driven centrifugal pump, to be installed at an estimated cost of £280. This operated automatically, presumably through a float switch, whenever a certain volume of water was drained from the tank, via the water columns).

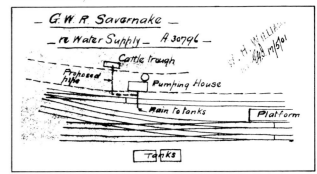

A later item from the files, dated 2nd July 1887, refers to an average of eleven GWR tender engines and seven tank engines taking water at the station on week days. This information was no doubt assiduously compiled, so that engines from the M&SWJ line which might have used the facilities - at this time no details are given of these - could be charged accordingly. A later document from the Accountant's Office at Paddington, dated 6th July 1895, states that the M&SWJ were being charged 3d per tank for water taken by their engines at Savernake. Paddington raised the question as to whether this figure should be increased as engines with larger water capacity were now in use. A census taken shortly afterwards revealed that after all only one large tender engine was recorded and consequently no change was suggested.

The same file relates that in the same year, 1895, the diversion of fish trains over the Berks & Hants route had increased the need to pump water, to six hours during the day with a further three hours at the night. It was suggested that this could be reduced if a second water tank were provided and that suitable redundant tanks were available from either Bath - 8,300 gallons, or Oxford - 21,000 gallons. At the same time the traffic department was pressing for an additional water column to be sited at the west end of the station so that the branch engine could take water without transgressing onto the main line. (Swindon corrected this statement slightly; the spare tanks were in fact available at Bath and *Briton Ferry*). An entry for 1898 further relates that 'the two open tanks at Savernake should be covered over.'

Station water came from the canal for many years and where taps existed the standard 'Not drinking water' signs were located. An interruption in this supply is reported around July 1915 through the water level of the canal having dropped; this in turn was due to the pumps at Crofton having ceased work, owing to a lack of coal.

Commencing at an unknown date water was also supplied by the GWR to the proprietor of the *Savernake Forest Hotel* who in 1928 is reported as a Mr. Bain. Bearing in mind the doubtful quality of certain of the supplies obtained from Savernake it is interesting to speculate where this was obtained and what the hotel used it for.

SIGNALLING

Records of the first signal boxes erected on the GWR and the lines worked by it are sparse generally; Savernake is no exception and much of the information on its first years must be conjecture. It is reasonable to assume that prior to the Marlborough branch opening, in 1864, a small box was

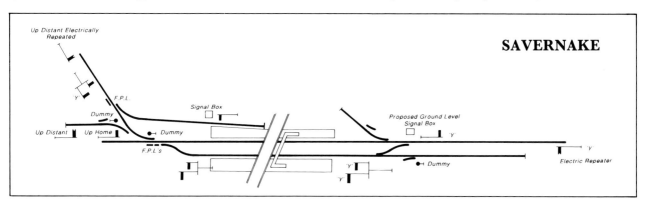

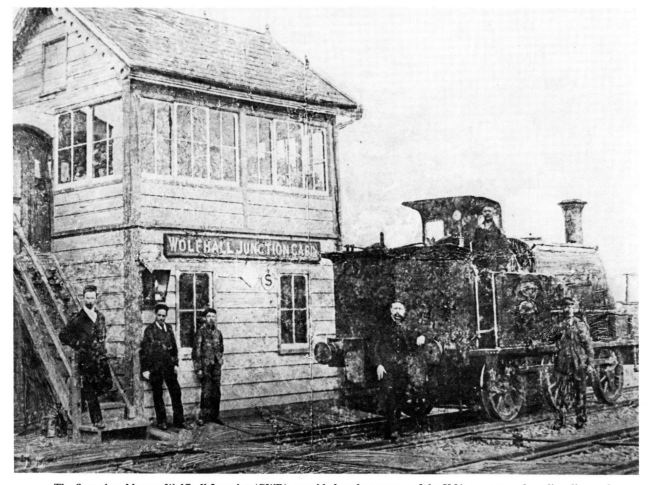

The first signal box at Wolfhall Junction (GWR), provided at the expense of the SMA company whose line diverged south from the Berks and Hants Extension at this point. Built to the design of the Gloucester Carriage and Wagon Co, it remained in use until at least 1898 and as discussed in the text, possibly a while longer. Despite its non-Great Western appearance the box may well have contained a GWR locking frame, whilst certain minor details, notably the 'S' and 'T' plates are pure Great Western. Standing on the up main line is *Grosvenor* a Hunslet 0-6-0T of 1884. Acquired by Messrs. Pauling in 1898 it was used in the doubling of the Berks and Hants through Savernake, and thereby assists in dating the photograph at around 1898/9. Notice the bridge rail still in place on the main line. The fate of the signal box after 1899 is not recorded.

Swindon Society

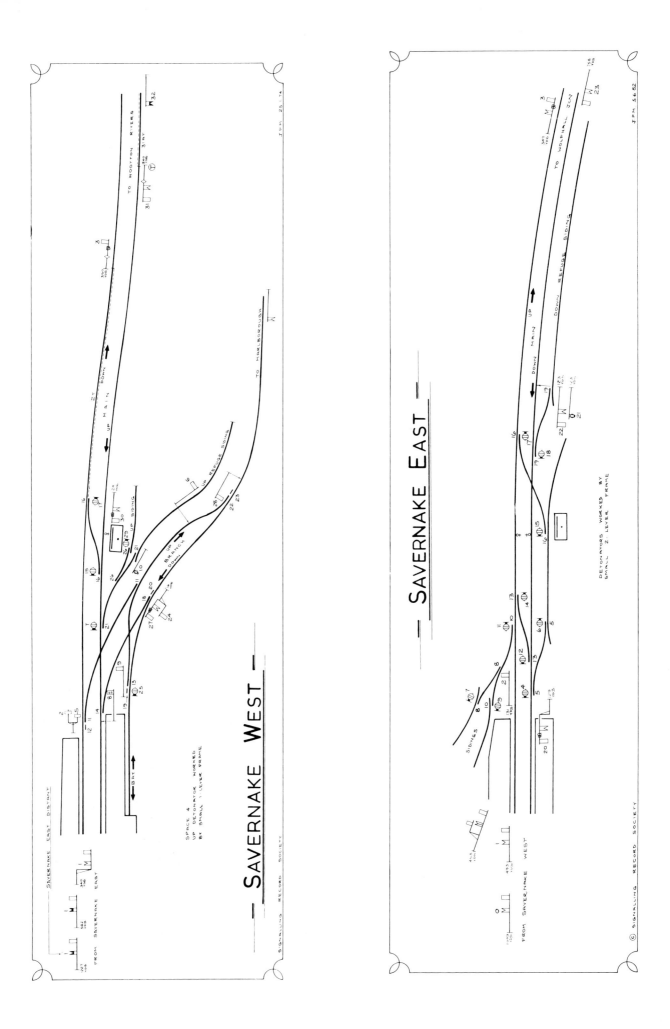

— SAVERNAKE WEST —

TO WOOTTON RIVERS

UP MAIN

DOWN

TO MARLBOROUGH

UP REFUGE SIDING

UP SIDING

UP BRANCH

DOWN

BAY

SPACE 4
UP DETONATOR WORKED
BY SMALL LEVER FRAME

SAVERNAKE EAST DISTANT

FROM SAVERNAKE EAST

JPM 25/74

© SIGNALLING RECORD SOCIETY

— SAVERNAKE EAST —

TO WOLFHALL JCN

DOWN MAIN

UP

DOWN REFUGE SIDING

SIDINGS

DETONATORS WORKED BY
SMALL 2 LEVER FRAME

FROM SAVERNAKE WEST

JPM 5 82

© SIGNALLING RECORD SOCIETY

GREAT WESTERN RAILWAY.

OPENING OF
NEW GOODS STATION at SAVERNAKE

The Great Western Railway Company's

NEW GOODS STATION

AT

SAVERNAKE

(ADJOINING THE PASSENGER STATION)

WILL BE OPENED ON

JUNE 15th, 1903,

FOR

Coal and Coke, Grain, Timber, Bricks, Stone, Hay and Straw, and other descriptions of Merchandise & Mineral Traffic.

Accommodation is provided for dealing with Horses, Carriages and Furniture Vans.

Information respecting Rates, and other arrangements, can be obtained on application to the Company's Station Agent at Savernake, or to Mr. W. Sparks, District Goods Manager, Reading.

PADDINGTON STATION, JUNE, 1903.　　**J. L. WILKINSON**, General Manager.

WYMAN & SONS, Ltd., Printers, Fetter Lane, London, E.C., and Reading.—6570a.

A rear view of Savernake East signal box with a collection of short wheeled based vehicles occupying at least part of the mileage siding. The signal box is known to have had a 23 lever frame in 1899 which was later extended to 24. On the main line are what appear to be a pair of 4-wheeled brake composite vehicles, although it is not possible to identify if they are painted in brown livery of 1908 or the crimson lake colour scheme used from 1912. The 502 yards canal tunnel at Savernake marked the highest point of the waterway between London and Bristol at 457ft above sea-level. The pumping house at Crofton, just east of Savernake, was required to pump continuously to maintain the requisite water level which might well have dropped owing to lock use.

N.R.M.

Wolfhall Junction, as arranged after 1933, at which time the single line branch was in effect extended south so that a passing loop was available. By this time the original requirements for goods transfer at Wolfhall had been removed, the GWR having absorbed the former MSWJ system in 1923. To the rear of the signal box can be seen a single siding, though there is some evidence to suggest that at one time a second, short one, may also have existed. In the background and just visible above the roof of the box it is just possible to make out the top of the former MSWJ signal box of the same name, retitled at the time this photograph was taken (the mid-1950s), *Grafton South Junction.*

T.B. Sands

provided; a reference within official GWR records that in September 1863 the sum of £29 10s and 5d was incurred in '.....moving signals at Savernake'.

A signal box is shown on the down side of the main line, on a plan of 1877, just west of the road overbridge. No other information on this first box has been uncovered. By 1879 a replacement structure had been provided on the opposite side of the railway just north of the bay platform and near to the actual junction of the branch with the main line. No photographs or plans of the building have been found although it is known to have had a brick base with the operating floor, presumably, positioned above. Likewise the number of levers is not reported and it is unlikely that few, if any, instruments were contained within. No interlocking existed between the points and signals, this primitive arrangement persisting until the box was replaced. Expenditure of £211 on telegraph working for the main line had been authorised in early 1864 using Spagnoletti instruments although as recounted previously it is possible the equipment was not brought into use until some time later. The instruments were situated in the station buildings and so were under the direct supervision of the station master.

The situation remained basically unaltered until the changes to the track layout brought about by the coming of the SMA line in 1882/3. At that time the second signal box was closed and two replacement signal boxes built, one at either end of the station. That at the Pewsey end of the station was named Savernake West and was located in the 'V' of the Marlborough branch junction.

With the passing loop at the station extended eastwards towards Reading the points at that end were now beyond the limit of mechanical control from the new west box. A second box was thus provided 462 yards east - 'Savernake East,' located on the south side of the main lines and the new down goods loop. Both were to the same design and were fitted with a double twist type of locking frame. Brickwork was used for the lower floor and rear wall and timber for the front and sides on the operating floor.

It is interesting to speculate for a moment as to why two substantive boxes were provided at this time, instead of one being a ground level cabin as per the original 1879 proposals, described earlier. Possibly the GWR already had thoughts concerning a future upgrading of the main line and as such were making provision for this very early on.

The signal box at Wolfhall Junction is believed to date from 25th March 1882 and was provided to control the junction with the SMA south from Savernake towards Andover. Originally single line at this point, a loop was provided in the Berks and Hants here from which a double junction led south onto SMA metals. The SMA itself became single after a short distance. The signal box stood on the north side of the main line, a wooden structure provided by the Gloucester Carriage & Wagon Co. It contained an unspecified type and size of lever frame although it is known that there were 18 working levers. From contemporary correspondence it would appear at least one sizeable transfer siding was provided at Wolfhall, presumably alongside the connection between the two systems. This assumption is based on earlier references to the construction of a transfer siding at the station - later called the canal siding - which would appear to have been a temporary arrangement until facilities at the junction were available.

Although unconfirmed, it is believed the signal box at Wolfhall Junction survived the closure of the physical connection between the GWR and M&SWJ systems at this point from 26th June 1898. It is thought to have finally closed in 1899 and may well have been at the time this section of the main line opened as double track. There are conflicting reports as to the situation with regard to the former connection between the GWR and M&SWJ at Wolfhall Junction from 1898 to about 1900. One source declares that a single siding left the GWR running towards the M&SWJ, terminating in a dead end beyond the canal bridge. Another source however implies this continued albeit disused, to form a trailing connection into the M&SWJ. It was controlled by a 3-lever ground frame.

What is certain is that the connection between the two

WOLFHALL JUNCTION

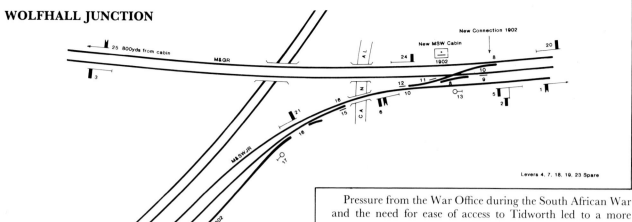

New Connection 1902

New MSW Cabin 1902

25 800yds from cabin

M&GR

M&SWJR

New Siding 1902

New GW Cabin 1902

Levers 4, 7, 18, 19, 23 Spare

Pressure from the War Office during the South African War and the need for ease of access to Tidworth led to a more permanent arrangement at the junction and a second exchange siding was added. This was known as Wolfhall siding with the costs of the new work reported at £1,000, the GWR and MSWJ each paying half. An agreement between the two ensured that the latter would pay the maintenance costs. At the same time signal boxes were provided at each end to control the new arrangements. To confuse the matter both were named Wolfhall Junction, one on the GWR and the other the M&SWJ. An official inspection by the Board of Trade took place on 25th July 1902 and the new works brought into use three days later on 28th July, worked by electric train staff. Again the initial cost of the apparatus, this time £1,100, was divided between the two concerns with maintenance undertaken by the M&SWJ. An undertaking as to the method of operating the single line was signed by the consenting parties on 9th November 1902.

systems was reinstated for wagon transfers from 1st November 1900, with the addition of a loop siding between the GWR main line and canal bridge. The methods of operating, particularly from the GWR side are not reported.

Although not strictly relevant to the text this view of Wolfhall Junction MSWJ, may help the reader to become a little more familiar with certain of the locations referred to in the text. On the left are the MSWJ lines leading north towards Marlborough, which after 1898 continued across the GWR main line on the route of the new Marlborough and Grafton line. The original connection to the GWR at Wolfhall Junction diverged just out of sight to the left although the junction signals for this are just visible. The line on the extreme left is a siding, trailing back from the connection between the GWR and original SMA connection, cut back to a point opposite the signal box in August 1928. To the right is the double line 'Grafton Curve' which allowed westbound GWR trains direct access onto the MSWJ. Most of the traffic using this link was destined for Tidworth. The signal box seen here was renamed 'Grafton South Junction' from 6th February 1933 and although in the ownership of the GWR from 1923 clearly shows its alien origin - being akin to the LSWR 'centre pillar' design.

Mowatt Collection

Grafton East Junction Signal box with the GWR main line running left to right towards Savernake and the 1905 connection to the MSWJ system curving away to the left. There is a suggestion that the signal box here may have been known as Grafton Junction at the time it was first opened. This however is refuted by the official GWR 1911 list of 'Stations, Signal Boxes etc.' where the name *Grafton Curve* is used. The anomaly is likely to have arisen due to the entry in the GWR Working Time books for 1904/5 which state that: *during the construction of the Grafton Curve, the 5.40 a.m. ex-Bristol Goods will call at* **Grafton Jct.** *(author's emphasis) when required* - presumably this was to deliver materials. Grafton East Junction signal box measured 21ft x 12ft x 8ft to the operating floor and contained a 21 lever frame at 5½ centres, with stud interlocking.

T.B. Sands

In connection with the 1933 changes in the Savernake area, the former M&SWJ signal box at Wolfhall Junction was renamed Grafton South Junction, with effect from 6th March 1933. In later years the single running line between Wolfhall Junction and Grafton South was operated on the 'acceptance lever' system.

The new GWR Wolfhall Junction signal box was built on the opposite side of the line to its former namesake and thus commanded a good view around the outside of the curve to the main line. It was to a standard GWR wooden design of the time; its dimensions were 19ft x 11ft x 7ft to the operating floor. Inside was a double twist type locking frame of 26 levers at 5¼ inch centres.

Though moving further away from Savernake it is necessary to make a brief mention of the next signal box eastwards as this too played its part in the complicated history of the railway layout at Savernake. This box was at Grafton and controlled a double line connection from the GWR Berks and Hants Extension line running south west to a double junction into the M&SWJ system just south of its Wolfhall Junction. (The reader may well find it of benefit to refer to the simplified layout of the area at this point in the text). Speculation exists as to the reason behind the construction of the Grafton Curve with two suggestions possible. The first of these is pressure from the War Office for a more direct connection from the GWR although a contributory factor may well have been the desire of the GWR itself to ensure a proportion of Tidworth bound traffic passed over its metals rather than using the LSWR system to Andover. (GWR trains working either via Wolfhall Junction or Grafton would still have to reverse at Ludgershall on the M&SWJ in order to gain access to the Tidworth branch itself).

The 44 chain Grafton Curve was authorised by the GWR Act of 15th August 1904 (much of which is taken up with powers for the Swansea District Lines); though a contract for construction worth £5,849 4s 6d was dated slightly earlier, 22nd July 1904. This was awarded to A. Jackaman & Son.

Progress on the new link was rapid with the M&SWJ monthly Engineer's reports recording that by 30th October 1904 a temporary connection between the two systems had been put in, to permit the removal of spoil from the new works. This was controlled by a ground frame on the main line; when the key for the ground frame was removed it locked the main line running signals. It is believed the temporary arrangements were in use for about four months.

The new connection opened on 6th September 1905 although the controlling signal box on the south side of the GWR main line, Grafton Curve box, had opened slightly earlier, from 6th July 1905. The box itself was a standard GWR brick structure typical of a number located throughout the system. It housed a 21 lever frame with stud locking, the levers set at 5¼ inch centres. Dimensions were 21ft x 12ft x 8ft to the operating floor. An official inspection of the new works by the Board of Trade took place on 7th September 1905.

Closure of the M&SWJ Wolfhall Junction box is associated with the opening of the Grafton Curve, and a replacement was provided on a new site some yards south of the previous structure. This controlled the new double line junction from Grafton GWR. One effect was that direct mechanical operation of the turnouts from the M&SWJ towards the GWR at Wolfhall was now beyond the acceptable limit of mechanical interlocking; instead these were controlled by a ground frame, unlocked by a key on the electric train staff working the line between the two Wolfhall Junction signal boxes.

On the main line track circuiting was authorised at Savernake on 30th July 1914, at a cost of £650, part of an expenditure of £50,000 on a number of locations with similar equipment. Around the same time self acting catch points were installed on the main line near the station in both directions, 640 yards outside the up home for Savernake West and a similar distance from the Savernake East down home signal. This afforded protection in the event of a coupling break which would otherwise have allowed vehicles to run back towards either Burbage or Wolfhall.

Plans were also made for a consolidation of the signalling arrangements at Savernake station, dating from 12th January 1937. This would have involved just one signal box in replacement for the east and west boxes. The new box, 33ft x 12ft, was to have been sited near to the existing west box and would have contained a 64 lever frame including 8 spare levers. Minor alterations to the interlocking of the neighbouring boxes at Burbage Goods and Wolfhall Junction would have been required. The work, probably proving too expensive or overtaken by war, was not proceeded with.

The working arrangements for the block sections at the time the main line was still single track are of interest:

Form and colour of staff and ticket, July 1881:

Bedwyn-Savernake; square, red.
Savernake-Pewsey; round, white.

From March 1883:

Bedwyn-Wolfhall Junction; triangular, red.
Grafton SMA-Wolfhall Junction; round, green.
Wolfhall Junction-Savernake East; square, blue.
Savernake West-Pewsey (double line between Savernake East and Savernake West); round, white.

BURBAGE WHARF

Slightly less than one mile west of the station at Savernake was Burbage Wharf, which deserves mention through importance in the siting of Savernake passenger station.

Despite its apparent insignificance it has proved possible to uncover an amount of information on the location. This is found as early as 19th April 1861 with a minute of the Berks and Hants Extension Company, showing that at the Directors' meeting of that date an application was read from a Mr. Brooks asking for permission to construct a siding at his own cost. This was agreed subject to a satisfactory arrangement as to the details.

Whether this was ever completed is uncertain although what is clear is that at the previous Directors' meeting the decision had finally been taken as to the siting of the passenger station at Savernake.

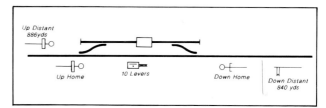

The buildings at Burbage appeared at the same time as the construction of the main line although unlike the passenger stations the cost is not reported. There was a brick 'Goods warehouse' with slate roof approximately 45ft x 35ft with a single loop siding through, onto the main line.

Croxteth Hall **on a down 'Class A' working, heading for Savernake past Grafton East Junction box. Notice the ATC ramp on the up line of the curve and the whistle board which applied to trains leaving it to join the main line. Behind the box are the remains of the 1913 siding, installed for a banking engine (to assist trains up the final section of the climb to Savernake) and also to unload coal for Crofton Pumping Station. A metalled way together with fencing gates and approach road was also provided at the same time. The new works were first authorised on 10th July 1913, at an estimated cost of £265, the final account being somewhat higher, £299.19s.3d to the engineering department and a further £121.18s.5d to the signal department. Regretfully there is no evidence to suggest the extent to which the banking engine was used, or any hint as to the volume of coal traffic for the pumping station. The late railway historian T.B. Sands has suggested that there was never any regular traffic over the 44 chain Grafton Curve; that its purpose was primarily for military traffic destined for Tidworth. There is a suggestion however that on busy Newbury race days it served to turn engines via the triangle of lines which now existed at this point. GWR locomotives would work Tidworth trains as far as Ludgershall - a little over 8 miles from the GWR main line. A reciprocal arrangement allowed MSWJ engines to work through Savernake GWR as far as Devizes or Westbury. This was based on an agreement between the two companies dated 30th October 1901.**

B.Y. Williams

Access to the goods station was effected via a gated road leading from the main road to Marlborough through Savernake Forest and hard by the Burbage Canal Wharf. Earliest located plans for the site are dated 1877 and show a stub siding at each end of the goods loop. It is known that later on a brick office existed at the west end of the goods shed which was built of the same material and measured approximately 12ft x 8ft. There was also a corrugated iron office 6ft x 3ft and at the east end a lean-to building 9ft 6ins x 7ft 6ins, in wood with a corrugated iron roof. It is not clear if these smaller buildings were original features.

By 1877 a small signal box was provided for the points leading off the single line although this was not a block post. The single line section ran from Savernake to Pewsey. The Board of Trade inspected the Berks and Hants line from Hungerford to Holt Junction on 3rd May 1877 and the report reveals the signal box to have contained 10 levers including 2 spares with interlocking between the points and signals. A basic diagram of the location reveals the existence of up and down line signals with the down distant the only one with a semaphore arm.

In 1900 in connection with the doubling of the main line, a replacement signal box was provided. This was necessary as the site of the old box was required for the new down line but little is known of this new structure. The suggestion has been made that it was second hand, a leftover from Devizes following the rebuilding of that station. One item transferred from the old to the new box was the nameplate, which read 'Burbage Siding Signal Box'; this had been ordered from Reading in October/November 1897.

The new double track main line made little difference to the siding access with trailing connections available from the up and down main. This layout made a single compound crossing into the up main line necessary, at the east end of the yard. A connection was thus available between the up and down lines.

By 1922 the facilities had reached their peak with cattle pens on the stub siding at the east end; a loading gauge stood at the west end of the goods shed whilst there were also two cranes, one of 5 tons capacity on an area of hard standing outside the shed and a smaller one and a half ton capacity crane within the shed.

Originally conceived both as an interchange point for goods between the railway and canal and for unloading goods destined for Marlborough, both activities diminished with the decline of the Kennet and Avon Canal and opening of the Marlborough branch. Traffic afterwards was very much local in its character. The goods station was important, for comparable arrangements did not exist at nearby Savernake although this of course changed from 1898 onwards.

As might be expected, the train service to the siding was fairly spasmodic, although back in January 1863 it was reported that one daily goods train each way called at Burbage, 9.20 a.m. in the down direction and 3.15 to 3.30 p.m. in the up direction. By May 1864 an additional down mixed train was reported calling at about 6.50 a.m.

The meagre traffic was mainly coal received and agricultural traffic which was forwarded. Livestock was also despatched. The GWR Traffic Statistics covering the period 1903-1933 receipts show a peak at £3,722 in 1923; by 1932 these had fallen to £1,280. The following year, 1933, receipts amounted to just £651.

With such a limited amount of traffic it is perhaps a wonder the facilities survived as long as they did; closure did not occur until 15th December 1941 although officially Burbage was still open at this time for 'Station to Station' traffic. Final closure took place from 10th November 1947, possibly as an accounting exercise, for there had been little movement of goods for some time prior to this. The cost of removal of the various permanent way fixings, etc. was reported at £1,225.

The signal box survived until 11th April 1948 though it was likely to have been switched out for some time prior to this. One of the few official references to the site appears in the 1931 Appendix to the working timetable.....*shunting must cease on the up line or from the up line to and from the goods siding whenever a passenger train has been signalled to pass in the down direction.*

The final part of the story of Burbage Goods Station came in September 1956 when the former goods shed was leased to a firm of agricultural machinery suppliers. This agreement continued until September 1965. The site was finally cleared by Messrs. Fairclough & Co. on behalf of the Western Region in November 1967.

The only view so far located of Burbage Goods Station, looking westwards from the A345 road overbridge in 1922. The Kennet and Avon Canal lies partly hidden to the right of the access road and goods shed building. From the 'off' position of the various main line signals it may well have been that the signal box was switched out for long periods even at this early time. The actual box was located at 70m 76ch from Paddington and was afforded the official reference number 535. Records show that in 1886 a Mr. W. Webber was in charge at the site whilst a July 1906 rating assessment reveals that during that month 311 goods trains used the main line here, none either commencing or terminating at the siding.

CHAPTER SIX
THE TERMINUS AT MARLBOROUGH

The terminus at Marlborough was located slightly south east of the town in the parish of Preshute, in a field known as the 'Cherry Orchard.' This was to the west of the main Marlborough to Burbage road - nowadays the A346. The single passenger platform ran approximately east-west and together with the main station buildings, lay on the north side of the line.

Marlborough High Street and the centre of the town were approximately one mile from the railway by road, although a considerably shorter route was by way of a footpath known as Isbury Lane. This pathway led directly into the station yard to continue across the lines and thence into open country, in the general direction of Savernake.

The access road to the station, on a steep slope in keeping with the local terrain, perpetuated the name of Cherry Orchard rather than the more usual Station Road. It very quickly opened out into the station yard with the main buildings straight ahead. The site of the station was in effect a small plateau overlooking the town to the north with (on the south side) a small valley, at the bottom of which the A346 road curved round on the initial stages of its climb of Postern Hill and eventually to Savernake Forest. The station was thus somewhat exposed to the elements and well in keeping with the tradition that railway stations were cold and draughty places.

Put up by the contractors Dalrymple and Findley, the original cost of the station building is recorded as £788 or 'nine and one third pence' per cubic foot. In plan form the passenger building described an 'L' shape with a total floor area of 999 sq. ft. The design was in contemporary gothic style; red brick was used for the walls with freestone quoins under a slate roof. Externally it measured 44 ft long by 27ft 3ins (maximum) and 18ft 3ins (minimum) wide. Inside were the usual facilities, including a booking office which probably also served as the station master's office, general waiting room, first class waiting room and ladies waiting room. There was also a small store room and toilets.

Unusually the booking office and general waiting room were in effect contained within the same area, rendering it easily the largest room in the building. Separating the two was a curved counter of 'L' shape which apparently suffered from having an open access-way at one end. Security then seems not to have been an urgent consideration.

Entry to the station from the approach yard was via a substantially panelled wooden door with the exit to the platform via a similarly proportioned door located virtually opposite. Draughts then within the building must have been prodigious. Heating for this area was provided from an angled fireplace and with another smaller fireplace behind the booking office counter.

At each end of the 'L' of the building was a small bay window beneath a domed, although still essentially flat, roof. The curvature was not visible due to a small parapet.

Leading off the general waiting room and to the left of the main entrance from the station yard was the first class waiting room. This was small in size being only 8ft 7ins x 12ft, though no doubt it proved adequate for most occasions. Access was from a door leading from the general waiting room, whilst a further

Marlborough Station, 23rd. May 1929 and Henry Casserley's classic view of the branch train at the station. The central figure outside the signal box is guard Bill Beale a former MSWJ signalman who transferred duties following grouping. In the background it is possible to discern an open wagon outside the engine shed and presumably for the disposal of ash.

H.C.Casserley

A 1950s view of the main buildings and 20 years since the termination of passenger traffic. Notice the small slit window at the end of the building. Just visible to the extreme left and on the platform, is the lamp hut. It would seem that the spear fencing around the station site may have been moved after 1933.   *T.B. Sands*

door led to the ladies waiting room and wc. One can imagine therefore in by-gone days, the situation whereby a third class female passenger would have to pass through the first class area in order to reach the w.c.! A further angled fireplace and back-to-back with the one in the booking office afforded warmth in the first class area.

Over the bay windows in each gable end of the building were two small slit windows, although interestingly these do not feature on the original plans. They can be seen in photographs elsewhere in the book.

Access to the male w.c. and urinals was from outside but not under the protection of the platform canopy. This latter feature was 12ft wide by 44ft long and ran the entire length of the building extending slightly over the rails. It was composed of 'fir rafters' supported on five cast iron columns bearing longitudinals and boarded over with 1½ins timber. From under the canopy it was also possible to gain access to the small store room located at the east end of the building

At the eastern end of the platform were the cattle pens, with direct access from the station yard. An early plan dated 22nd December 1881, however, indicates the cattle pens as being slightly on the Savernake side of the goods shed. There is no proof of their existence on this site and the plan is probably only a proposal.

Just east of the main building and still on the platform was a corrugated iron lamp hut, whilst on the opposite side of the cattle pens and at the bottom of the platform ramp stood a platelayers hut. At an unknown date but possibly around late 1904 a small shed was erected adjacent to the cattle pens and used as a store hut for the GWR road motor services.

At the west or Savernake end of the main platform was a loading bank angled away from the running line with both end-on and side-loading facilities. This was reached by two sidings, a short one which led directly off the running line and another leading from the goods shed. In days past it had been the practice for the gentry to take with them their own horse drawn carriage when travelling by train - this is where such vehicles were loaded.

The road entrance to the goods yard was adjacent to the loading bank and was guarded by the usual weighbridge and hut.* The goods shed was of conventional design with a single through siding and unloading platform on the north side. The building was approximately 54ft long by 34ft wide - scaled from plans. At the station end was a lean-to office and on the loading platform a hand operated 30cwt capacity crane. Regretfully no details as to this building's construction or photographs of it have been traced, although it would appear to have been similar to that erected at Burbage Wharf and would certainly date from about the same time.

Beyond the goods shed there is some evidence that at one time a crossover existed back into the main line, although it has not proved possible to date this feature. A number of coal staithes existed alongside the continuation of the goods yard siding; at the end of which stood another platelayers hut.

Isbury Lane footpath crossed the railway between the goods shed and the passenger station and passage was protected by the usual statutory warning boards.

Just prior to entering the platform the running line was split by means of a three-way turnout; the left hand portion led to the loading dock mentioned earlier whilst straight ahead was the passenger platform. To the right the track led off in the form of a loop siding which continued towards the engine shed as well as

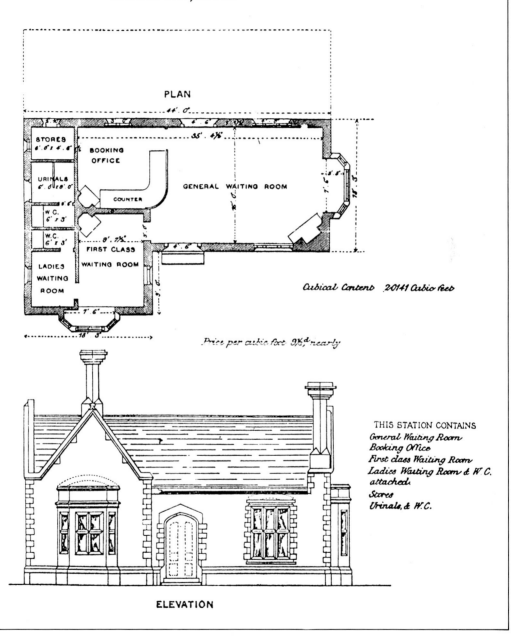

Passenger Building Total Cost £788.0.0

This includes an awning 12' wide and 44' long, composed of fir rafters 9" x 3", supported on 5 cast iron columns, bearing Longitudinals 7" x 2½ and boarded over with 1½' boarding.

A Gothic Structure, Walls of Red brick, with Freestone Quoins &c, and a slate roof.

Total Area 999 square feet

PLAN

STORES
6'.6 x 4'.6

BOOKING OFFICE

URINALS
6'.6 x 10'.0

W.C.
6' x 3'

W.C.
6' x 3'

LADIES WAITING ROOM

COUNTER

GENERAL WAITING ROOM

FIRST CLASS WAITING ROOM

Cubical Content 20141 Cubic feet

Price per cubic foot 9½d nearly

ELEVATION

THIS STATION CONTAINS
General Waiting Room
Booking Office
First class Waiting Room
Ladies Waiting Room & W.C. attached.
Stores
Urinals, & W.C.

affording access by another crossover back into the platform line. Beyond the platform the track continued a short distance past the engine shed and water tank before ending abruptly at a set of buffer stops immediately above the cutting bearing the A346 road. The station was 5 miles 50 chains from Savernake and 75¼ miles from Paddington.

Unusually there were two loading gauges at the station, the first in the conventional position over the siding at the east end of the goods shed and the second over the run round loop almost opposite the station signal box - the signalling arrangements at the station are discussed in detail later in the chapter. It is believed few major changes, not even the gauge conversion of 1874, affected the track layout over the years.

Official records state the weighbridge had a capacity of 10 tons on a plate 11ft x 6ft. A GWR circular dated 1st February 1908 contradicts this, stating that at Marlborough 'no railway weighbridge is available for weighing the company's traffic.'

2-4-0 Metro tank No. 1499, on the crossover connecting the run round loop with the extension from the passenger platform. This engine was officially allocated to Marlborough at several periods in 1929 although not at the time the photograph was taken, 23rd May 1929! The high and somewhat ornate water tank dating from 1879 can be seen in the background; on the left is a permanent way hut and on the extreme right is the ash bunker. The water column was removed in 1934 at the time the engine shed was converted into a motor garage.

H.C. Casserley

The Locomotive Department

The single road engine shed stood at the east end of the siding, on a continuation of the run-round loop. The building dated from the opening of the station and until June 1874 had been home to the broad gauge engines working the line. The shed was constructed with brick side walls and wooden ends under a slate roof. The roof beams were of timber and formed a gable at either end of the structure. The beams also supported an internal smoke trough vented by two chimneys towards the front of the shed. Access was at the west end via two double doors. A pedestrian access door was also provided, to one side of these. As built the structure measured 50ft in length.

By 1892 a wooden extension had been added at the rear of the shed bringing the total length to 69ft. The reasons for this are not reported although it may well be that this was the time it was decided to allocate a second engine to Marlborough; the additional sheltered area would allow both locomotives to be brought under cover. No doors were provided at the east end of the structure. Between the running rails inside the shed was an inspection pit 39ft 10ins long. Inside the shed was a small cabin and also a wrought iron furnace for sand drying. This latter feature was provided with a chimney on the south side.

The short length of line outside the shed leading into the run-round loop was also used for locomotives standing; it too boasted a pit though at 23ft 10ins it was shorter in length. It was used for ash dropping whilst unusually for the time a water tap was provided for damping purposes. This could well have been necessary due to the close proximity of the passenger station. Opposite the pit was a small iron bin described as a coal bunker on certain plans, though its location suggests it may have been a receptacle for ashes - shovelled from the pit probably by the night cleaner who would also have been responsible for the furnace in the sand drier.

Between the engine shed road and the extension of the platform line stood the ubiquitous GWR water crane, fed from an elevated water tank located opposite the engine shed. The extension of the platform line is also described as having been used for 'standing engines' and indeed beneath the aforementioned water tank was a wooden coaling stage. This was probably little more than a platform of old sleepers and measured 29ft 4ins x 11ft 4ins. The arrangements for the delivery of locomotive coal to the station are not reported but would no doubt be a single wagon at a time via the branch goods service. This wagon was then stabled alongside the coaling stage and unloaded by hand. (It is likely unloading was spread over a half day period). Up to 1879 locomotives would have been coaled manually although in that year a small hand operated crane which could be used to lift full baskets or tubs of coal into the waiting engines bunker, was installed on the platform. Correspondence from Swindon states that '.. the crane is similar to that about to be fixed at Salisbury'; at the same time a replacement water tank was installed.

Near to the coal stage and water tower was a wooden pump house with gable roof, containing a steam pump for lifting water into the tank. Generally the latter was replenished twice weekly with power provided by the branch engine, the driver removing the engine's whistle, connecting up a pipe and tying the whistle chain down. In this way steam would be available to drive the pump though such an operation was notorious for its not inconsiderable use of steam from the locomotive boiler.

From 1902 until the shed closed in 1933 details of the engines allocated to Marlborough are given in a series of records compiled at Swindon. These are shown in Appendix 1

A 1912 survey has also survived giving details as to how the locomotive power at Marlborough was utilised during the six days ended 16th January. Two engines were allocated during

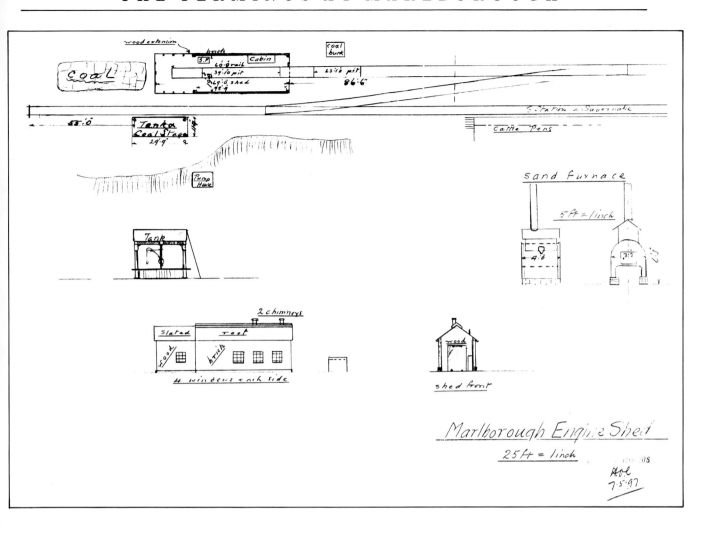

Seen from the MSWJ route, a clear view of the engine shed at Marlborough, with the pre-1892 wooden extension at the rear.

B.Matthews

GREAT WESTERN RAILWAY. LOCOMOTIVE DEPARTMENT.

Particulars of Shed and other accommodation for Running Engines at ___Marlborough___ *Station.*

ENGINE SHED (Sketch Plan to be attached).

How built (Stone, Brick or Wood) — Brick & wood   slate roof

Inside dimensions:
Length — 69·0
Breadth — 19·9
Height to top of roof ridge — 23·3
Do. do. wall plate — 16·7
Cubical contents —

Style of Roof (Gable, Hip Gable or Saw-tooth) — Gable
Roof principals (Material) — Wood
If fitted with Smoke Troughs — One over pit only
Date built, or date Shed was first used — –
Length of each Line used for running Engines — One 60·9
Do. do. do. repairs — None
Engine Pits—length of each used for running Engines — One 39·10
Do. do. do. repairs — None

SHOPS OR OFFICES OUTSIDE THE SHED.

	Pump house Wood	Coal Brick Iron
How built (Stone, Brick or Wood)		
Length	8·3	10·0
Breadth	6·6	7·0
Height to top of roof ridge	9·6	7·0
Do. do. wall plate	7·3	6·0
Cubical contents	None	
Style of Roof (Gable, Hip Gable or Saw-tooth)	Gable	Lean to
Roof principals (Material)		
Date built, or date opened		
Length of Line used for repairs		
Do. Engine Pit used for repairs		

OUTSIDE SHED.

Lines available for standing Engines — In front of shed 86·0   Behind coal stage 55·0
Engine Pits—length of each — One 23·10
Do. at Station — None

ENGINE TURNTABLES.

Diameter —
Length of Rail —
Girders (Material) —
How turned — None
Where fixed —
Date fixed —
Maker —

COAL STAGE.

Sketch and size — 29·6 x 11·6 platform underneath tank
Number of Cranes or Tips — One Crane
How built (Stone, Brick or Wood) — Wood on C.S. columns
Date built —

SAND FURNACE.

Outside dimensions — length, 4·0   breadth, 3·3   height 6·3
Brief description and Sketch — Wrought Iron
Date built —
Where situated — Out Inside Shed

Date Certified 7·5·97   W. H. Williams   Superintendent's Signature.
"   "   8·2·99   Per H.L.

From this view the close proximity of the GWR and MSWJ lines at Marlborough is apparent and it is also possible to detect the pathway - on the right and in front of the engine shed - used by staff for access between the two stations.
Adrian Vaughan Collection

Taken some years after the shed had ceased to be used for locomotive purposes, with several changes visible. Amongst these are the filled-in ash pit and sleeper and tarmacadam roadway leading to the shed. To the right and to the rear was a small group of terraced cottages, provided by the MSWJ for their own staff. Access to these was either from a footpath off the Marlborough to Burbage road or via another footpath alongside the MSWJ line, where it crossed the main road. One of these cottages was occupied by the MSWJ station master.

Adrian Vaughan Collection

this time.

60 hours at work 20.8% of period
35 hours standing 12.2% of period
27 hours on shed for locomotive purposes; preparing, coaling, steam raising, washing out, tube cleaning etc. 9.4% of period
2 hours under repair 0.7% of period
22 hours cleaning 7.6% of period
142 hours standing idle 49.3% of period
288 Total Engine Hours

The survey provided a comparison with two other sheds each with an allocation of two engines. Both of these recorded far better performances with regard to the percentage of time standing idle, namely Lambourn at 32.3% and Fairford at just 5.9%.

Official reports suggest that it was intended to close the shed in April 1929 but this was deferred. Closure eventually coincided with the withdrawal of the passenger service in March 1933 and accordingly the locomotive allocation to Marlborough ceased. Official reports state the closure to have been a 'temporary affair' but as far as the steam engine was concerned it was destined to become permanent.

The following year, 1934, Swindon produced plans to convert the former engine shed into a motor repair garage. This in itself would appear strange as it was already two years since the GWR had ceased its involvement in the bus service. Whilst the work appears to have been carried out, it also involved the removal of the water crane and covering of the outside engine pit with sleepers. In addition to this the permanent way hut at the east end of the station was removed whilst sleepers were also placed between the rails of the extension from the passenger platform. A tarmacadam roadway was laid from outside the

engine shed to the eastern end of the station yard. At this latter point a small wash down was provided.*

Water Supplies to the Station

Aside from the water crane mentioned previously, the tank also supplied the station urinals and w.c, as well as a tap at the cattle dock. It would appear that at the time of opening in 1864 a secondhand water tank had been erected, for just 14 years later in October 1878 correspondence passed between the Locomotive Carriage & Wagon Department at Trowbridge (of which Marlborough was then an outstation) and Swindon regarding a replacement.

One month later on 22nd November 1878 a further letter from Trowbridge recommended that a larger tank 28ft x 10ft x 5ft 6ins be provided. This contrasted with the original structure at 15ft x 10ft x 4ft 3ins. Swindon replied with approval for a replacement structure although clearly not with the speed the other departments may have wished. For on 2nd December 1878 a letter was written from the District Goods Manager's office at Reading stating '.. the stage of the water tank projects so far over the line as to prove dangerous to passing trucks... indeed during that month two wagon sheets were badly damaged.'

Although conjecture it is likely the intention was to establish an additional 'country lorry' service at Marlborough. As this occurred after the cessation of passenger services and demise of much of the original Marlborough Railway it is really beyond the scope of this book. Another alternative was to 'outbase' a vehicle from one of the neighbouring 'country lorry' stations.

This letter produced some action and for three days around 29th March 1879 the water supply to the station was cut off to facilitate the erection of the new tank. A further note expressed concern as to how this temporary interruption in supplies would adversely affect the use of the station toilets. Some months afterwards the steam pumps were removed for repair, which is likewise reported as causing some disruption. A further difficulty to the station supply was highlighted in 1899 due, it was stated, to the inefficiency of the pipe from the water tank. As a result a number of new outlet pipes were provided. In addition in 1909 further improvements were made which now included a supply to a hydrant within the engine shed as well as to an area of hardstanding near the cattle pens, used for the washing of GWR road vehicles.

There is no reference at all to a drinking water supply to the station and it would appear then that churns may have been used.

The water crane was removed in 1937 although at the same time a supply was connected to a 6ins stand pipe near to the up line of the former M&SWJ system. At this time the other supplies on the High Level site remained connected.

Changes over the Years

One of the first alterations to the layout at Marlborough took place on 21st February 1881, when an agreement was reached between the GWR* and the contractors for the Swindon Marlborough & Andover Railway, Messrs Watson Smith and Watson, for a siding on the south side of the station. This was so that materials for use in the construction of the new line might be unloaded and has already been referred to in detail in Chapter 4. It is not clear how long the siding remained in use - presumably only until the opening of the SMA as far as Marlborough in July 1881. In addition the land fell away

sharply in the area where the siding diverged and working arrangements would necessarily have been undertaken with some circumspection.

An agreement was signed between the various parties on 22nd December 1881, for a junction between the SMA and the Marlborough Railway just south of the latter's station, to allow SMA trains access to Savernake and their own route south towards Andover. The actual junction lay more or less adjacent to the platelayers hut at the Savernake end of the goods yard. In order to comply with existing requirements, the MR became double for a short length, a double junction veering away to the south east and the SMA station in the form of a loop 730ft long**. Cost of construction of this connection was estimated 'at £523 exclusive of earthworks, ballast and locking'. To control the new junction a signal box was provided, known as Marlborough South Junction.

*Although still an independent company in 1896, the Marlborough Railway was worked by the GWR and as such would have been party to any agreement which would affect traffic over the line. It is likely that standard GWR equipment in the form of notices, water crane, etc. were used on the line from the outset.

** The reader is again referred to the photograph accompanying Chapter 4 at this point, which affords an early view of the SMA Marlborough station. Although beyond the scope of the present volume it is interesting to discuss the connection to the SMA further; the original agreement clearly states it to be just 730 feet, not yards. The SMA route thus went from double line at the junction with the MR into single track and reverted to double line a short distance further on. What signalling arrangements may have existed at the SMA Marlborough station at this time can only be guessed at.

A panoramic view of both Marlborough stations and taken from Postern Hill. The photograph can be dated as pre-1892 as on this date a signal box was provided at the terminus. It must however be after 1882 as the connection exists between the GWR and SMA companies. In the foreground is the main Marlborough to Burbage road through Savernake Forest and with what may well be the former toll house - and which still survives today, at the bottom of the hill. Aside from the legendary connections with Merlin, the Town has a number of other famous sons including Cardinal Wolsey who was ordained at St.Peter's in March 1498, Thomas Hancock, who invented the india rubber process and his brother Walter, who invented the steam road engine.

Wiltshire Newspapers

The work was carried out by the GWR and inspection by the Board of Trade took place on 21st March 1882. The running of through trains however was delayed nearly a year until February 1883 as a result of the condition of facilities at Savernake, referred to earlier in this book. The junction survived until the opening of the Marlborough and Grafton line in 1896.

An entry in the minutes of the GWR Engineering Committee for March 1911 refers to the provision of an additional siding and loading bank at the station. Although there is no evidence to suggest these were ever carried out, it is believed a raised platform was provided within the goods yard, close to the location of the coal staithes. This measured 101ft 8ins x 37ft and may have had a form of cover added subsequently as the area was later used by 'The West of England Sack Co.'

Following the absorption of the former M&SWJ system into the GWR, the name of the terminus at Marlborough was suffixed by the words 'High Level' to avoid confusion with the other station in the town which in turn became 'Low Level'. These changes took effect from 1st July 1924.

It was not long before Paddington began to take a serious look at what was a glaring duplication of resources in the area, and as a first step to rationalisation the connection between the two lines, at what had been Marlborough South Junction, was reinstated. The connection was brought into use on 23rd November 1926 in a simpler form than had existed previously, a single lead from the running line falling away towards the up line of the former Marlborough and Grafton line.

Following closure to passenger services and abandonment of the central portion of the original Marlborough railway in 1933, the reinstated connection became the only means of access to the High Level site. From here freight continued to be dealt with until final abandonment in 1964.

Traffic

Passenger traffic at the station was, of necessity, fairly light although it is known a number of regular journeys were made by people who walked from the vicinity of Pewsey to Savernake before boarding the branch train for Marlborough. Presumably their employment lay within the latter town. An indication of the number of journeys can be gauged from the traffic statistics; from these it is seen that the number of tickets issued between 1903 and 1924 remained basically consistent at 20,000 per annum though a peak was reached at nearly twice that figure, 38,000, in 1913. This last figure however still only represents an average loading of six persons per train daily, based on the assumption of 10 trains each way over a six day week. Subsequent to 1924 the number of passengers declined steadily from nearly 18,000 in 1925 to 10,500 by 1930, with even this figure halved only two years later. A similar pattern is indicated with season ticket travel; in the last full year of operation, 1932, just over 2,000 season tickets were issued indicating, apart from school children, some form of commuter traffic. Apart from the college trains visitors and walkers would use the branch to reach both Marlborough and the area of Savernake Forest.

Parcels traffic handled was in proportion to other business and reached its peak in the years 1923/1925 at some 2,000 items, before settling down to a fairly consistent 1,000 to 1,100 items per annum. There was at one time a Receiving Office at the Ailesbury Arms in Marlborough, although this was only short lived, from March 1929 to March 1931. Likely enough a proportion of the parcels traffic originated from concerned parents, with boys at the College.

As far back as 1907 there was a cartage agent in the town and on 9th December of that year the GWR entered into an

Looking towards the terminus in 1923, with the yard apparently well filled with wagons. The signal is unusual in having a lattice post, a departure from standard GWR practice.

National Railway Museum

Overgrown but basically unaltered since closure. The washing hanging from the canopy supports would tend to suggest the building was being used as living accommodation.

W.A.Camwell

A late view of the cattle dock, which stood at the east end of the station. The former MSWJ route from Swindon Town to Marlborough was closed completely from 9th September 1961 although goods and parcels continued to be dealt with. At this time it is said that up to four goods trains daily would still serve what was in effect a terminus although this does appear to be generous provision, as from 19th May 1964 the Low Level station was relegated to coal workings only and finally closed to all traffic on 7th September. Following the closure, goods traffic for the station was handled at Woodborough, Pewsey having ceased to handle goods at the same time. College trains had in the meanwhile continued to run to the station via Savernake Low Level, with the last of these on 1st May 1964. The occasion was not without unintended drama; when the diesel locomotive attempted to run-round prior to the return journey it was derailed where the track had been lifted at the north end of the former Low Level station.

Lens of Sutton

A distant view of the engine shed in its new guise as road motor 'garage' with what appears to be a *Bedford* lorry. The shed was eventually demolished sometime prior to May 1964.

Lens of Sutton

An interesting view of shunting operations at the terminus with the branch engine setting off from the platform. Note the brake van is lettered 'Marlborough' as its home station. A reference in the 1931 sectional appendix authorised the use of a tow-rope at the station although, tantalizingly, further details are not given. A note in the passenger timetable stated that motor taxis from local garages would meet most trains whilst from October 1890 a supply of footwarmers was available to Marlborough passengers.

Mowat Collection

agreement with Joshua Watts Brooks of The Green, Marlborough, to act 'for the whole town'. On 28th March 1912 however the traffic committee records the following entry:

In view of the unsatisfactory nature of the arrangements for the cartage of goods and parcels traffic at Marlborough, the Great Western Railway Traffic Committee approved of notice being given to the Agent to terminate their agreement, with the company itself performing this work and to enable them to do so the committee approved the purchase of cartage equipment and the hiring of stabling equipment as follows:

2 horses at £55 each £110
3 sets of harness at £6 each £18
1 Goods Lorry £47
1 Light Lorry and Parcels Lorry £44
The employment of two-car men, the hiring of stabling accommodation at £21 per annum.
The annual cost to the Company will be £261.1s.0d

This arrangement lasted until 1921, when a further agreement was entered into, this time with Messrs William Free & Sons of 18/19 High Street, Marlborough, appointed on 21st June 1921 to operate '.. for a mile radius from the station'. This somewhat restricted area was extended on 24th August 1925 to include '..the vicinity of the Town'.

Goods traffic at the station is best described as mundane and included the typical items expected at a small branch line terminus. It was at the centre of a fairly prosperous agricultural area and indeed in the early days the railway had certainly influenced farming in the region. This resulted in a reduced demand for oats and beans - previously used for horses and instead more acreage was devoted to green crops.

Highlight of the agricultural year was the annual sheep fair in Marlborough, which took place in late summer. At this time the

railway was extremely busy not only with the movement of livestock but also with visitors to the event. This accounted (partly at least) for the movement of no less than 431 livestock wagons in 1913.

There is no conclusive evidence to suggest any substantial traffic in racehorses but it is fairly certain, nonetheless, that this type of trade did exist. There were a number of racing stables in the area, including the renowned facilities at nearby Manton village.

Coal was handled by a variety of local merchants over the years including Messrs Robins Lane and Pinnegar, and William Free. Coal traffic remained constant at around 5,000 tons annually for some years although it was subject to variation, depending upon the weather.

In addition there was a steady, if small, amount of mineral traffic which suddenly rose to over 12,000 tons in 1931, at a time when other traffic on the branch was diminishing. This it is believed may have been material for improvements to the nearby London - Bristol trunk road (nowadays the A4). As would be expected mineral traffic despatched was small

Evidence of additional traffic is found as early as August 1886 with a reference to Messrs Webb & Spring of Stroud, Gloucestershire who were granted permission to install a portable engine near to Marlborough station and which was connected to the GWR water supply. In return Messrs. Webb & Spring agreed to transport timber from Marlborough over GWR metals to the saw mills at Stroud, involving a tortuous route via Savernake and thence either Devizes or Newbury.

Staff

Early references to the staff at Marlborough are limited, one

Army service corps loading railway wagons, probably destined for the garrison at Ludgershall or Tidworth, at Marlborough in 1916. On the extreme left is a road wagon mounted on another rail vehicle and believed to belong to the local coal merchant and haulage contractor, R.J. Free. The photograph was taken on the siding at the Savernake end of the goods shed, with the footpath and stile indicating the crossing of the railway by Isbury Lane, visible between the wagons.

The west end of the station, showing two 5-plank wagons in the former carriage loading dock. Above the wagons it is possible to glimpse the loading gauge over the run round loop; to the right of this is the Marlborough (Low Level) signal box, opened in 1933 to coincide with the revised track layout and working arrangements to Savernake.

Michael Hale

GREET WESTERN RAILWAY.

Return showing cause of delay to UP PASSENGER TRAINS at _____ Station.
on _____ day, the 8 of _____ 18_ .

The Station Master must personally supervise the preparation of this return, sign it himself, and see that every train is entered which may be booked to start from or call at his Station which is delayed over time; and also any train which may be checked or stopped out of course at his Signals or Stations, giving the fullest explanation of all delays, and he must forward the return to the Divisional Superintendent as directed in Mr. Tyrrell's Circular No. 558, dated 21st April, 1884.

Waterlow Bros. & Layton, Limited, 24, Birchin Lane, London, E.C.

Train from starting-point.		Booked time at this Station.		Actual time at this Station.		Minutes Lost.			Explanation of delay to be given here as per instructions above.
Time.	From	Arr.	Dep.	Arr.	Dep.	Delays at Signals.	Overtime at this Station.	Delays Waiting Connecting Trains.	
7 5	Swindon	7 3		7 45	7 45	5			Waiting arrival of 6.30 Andover arr. 7 44 am
4 30	"	4 5		4 50	50	5			" " 4 31 pm Swindon arr. 5.0 pm
						Station			
12 35	Marlboro	12 35		13 41		6			Late arrival of 12. 14 pm + Snow
4 12	"	4 12		4 30		8			" " 3. 50 pm "
6 55	"	6 55		7 4		9			Waiting line clear. M 18th York in front. Taken up

Station Master. [See back for DOWN PASSENGER TRAINS.

of the first being that to engineman George Wride, whose record of time worked in May 1891 is reproduced. This is one of few references to the staff of the locomotive department at the station who probably consisted of a driver-in-charge, fireman and night cleaner. There were times, as we have seen, when two engines were shedded at Marlborough, though it is likely additional men were sent from Trowbridge to cover the extra duty when required. Similarly the engineering department (track) staff are not included in the numbers shown on the traffic statistics.

The Marlborough traffic department staff complement varies over the years and is shown as eight in 1903, eleven in 1913 and no less than twenty-three by 1923. Ten years later in the depths of the Depression this figure had decreased to just seven. Included in these totals were station master, booking clerk, porter, shunter and signalman (it is possible the latter grade was combined under the term 'porter - signalman'). There was also at least one guard, whilst it is known that in 1914 guard G.T. Allum and porter-guard W.C. Verney were in charge of most branch trains. It is not certain if the 'road motor' drivers and conductors were included in these figures but this is probably unlikely.

The *GWR Magazine* provides a useful if at times confusing list of staff changes over the years; an entry for 1916 declares clerk W.V. Edwards to have transferred to Pewsey whilst C.T. Wood a signal-porter at Savernake was promoted to signalman at Marlborough.* Another full time signalman at Marlborough - although at an unknown date, was Mr. V. Bodman. It is said that this last named individual was particularly adapt at catching the train staff at speed.

In the same year, 1916, the *Magazine* carried a photograph and note to the effect that Joshua Watts, a packer with the

engineering department at Marlborough for the previous two years had been killed in action whilst serving with the armed forces. This is almost the same name as the man who had been the first carrier to the railway from 1907 to 1912 and it may well have been that he had joined the GWR after the closure of his business.

During the following year 1917, W. Hillier, foreman at Marlborough, moved to Newbury and W. Tuck transferred from Yeovil as parcels porter. Mr. Tuck's stay was however fairly short as he, together with H. Beverall moved to Westbury in 1920 to take up positions as goods guards. 1918 brought about a change in the clerical staff at the station with W.G. Flew coming from Salisbury and H.W. Gowthorne moving from Hungerford.

The first year of peace, 1919, saw a series of somewhat puzzling changes involving signalling personnel. In April Messrs F.G. Liddiard and C. Clements, both signal-porters at Marlborough moved to Portland and Yeovil respectively and at the same time, W.A. Swallow, signalman at Marlborough, moved to a similar post at Upwey Junction. These transfers pose two questions; why the sudden movement of men to the Weymouth area and why are no replacements shown as moving

The terms 'signal-porter' and 'porter-signalman' are used equally by the GWR in their various publications. The position was designed for locations which did not warrant a full time signalman or where a relief signalman might be required for a short period only during the day, covering a gap perhaps between shifts. This was probably the case at Savernake where one of the boxes may not have been open for the full 24 hour period.

One of the very few views of the terminus looking back towards Savernake. The goods shed is visible as is the MSWJ route and 1926 connection between the two systems. The overgrown and unkempt nature of the former branch typifies the system as it appeared in 1947. On the right the coaches may well be messing accommodation for staff, consequent upon the relining of the Marlborough (MSWJ) tunnel in 1946. Notice also the inside keyed rail on the former branch run round loop.

Statement shewing ... George Wride of Marlborough was employed Running ... his ... Marlborough and Savernake. W.E. May 9th 1891.

(Running Time taken from Train Bills.) (... and Shunting Time taken from Mileage Ticket.)

Monday 4th					Tuesday 5th					Wednesday 6th					Thursday 7th					Friday 8th					Saturday 9th				

Summary for the Week

	HOURS
Total Hours on Duty	72.30
Time Running	16.51
Time Shunting (as p Vouchers)	15.0
Fixed Allowance Shunting 1½ hours p Diem	9.0 40.51
Time not actually Running	31.39
Sunday Duty ... the above)	6.0

to Marlborough? Possibly in the latter case the vacancies were filled from other staff at the station.

The next three years witnessed only two changes; S.T. Perry joined the Marlborough staff from Castle Cary in 1920 as a porter and in 1922 F.G. Smart left for Bristol as a relief porter. Mr. Perry's stay was destined to be brief as he moved on to Portishead in 1923.

Further changes took place in 1925 with R.S. Hole moving from Marlborough High Level to Highbridge and F.M. Lewis moving to the terminus from Savernake. The final entry occurs in the same year with G. Fisher coming to Marlborough High Level from Pewsey as signalman.

Details of the holder of the station master grade are scarce and information is only available from 1899 onwards. At this time Henry S. Kench was in charge although by 1907 the name of William Charles Hitchman appears in the records. Four years later in 1911 John E. Potter is in the post and by 1915 'George' Jackman - sometimes spelt Jakeman. Mr. Jackman was transferred to Newquay in 1924 following the abolition of the post at what was now the High Level station. On his departure he was presented with a silver cigarette case by his former colleagues.

From 30th July 1924 Mr. A.W. Bowd took over control of both Marlborough stations; he had previously been the station master at the Low Level site, since 1906. The final station master to have control over the branch prior to its closure to passenger services was Charles Wellington Broom. He took over both stations at Marlborough in 1927.

Other known staff members - though at unknown dates, were Messrs Pike and W. (Bill) Beale together with enginemen Gardner, Whatley, Beckinsale and Thompson. It is known that the last locomotive crew moved to Acton following the branch closure.

After 1933 staffing of the High and Low Level stations was integrated and it is no longer possible to differentiate changes affecting the former branch terminus alone.

It is not believed that there was any MR or GWR owned living accommodation for railway staff in Marlborough though it may well be that a house was rented for the use of the station master.

Signalling

Until 1882 there was no signal box at Marlborough and the working was controlled purely on the basis of an undertaking given to the Board of Trade that only one train in steam would be on the line at any one time. This arrangement persisted throughout broad gauge days although it may be assumed some form of 'staff with key' was in use, unlocking the points affording access to the sidings. A similar arrangement persisted from the time of conversion to narrow gauge in 1874 until the advent of the SMA route in 1881/2. It is likely at least one signal was provided at the terminus in each direction to control trains entering or leaving the station, possibly worked by a hand lever at the base of the post. An official GWR report on the interlocking of points and signals and dated 1880, declares the station at Marlborough to be amongst a number of locations on the system 'not locked', which can be taken to mean there was no interlocking between the points and signals. The former were also hand operated at this time.

With the provision of a double junction joining the branch with the SMA route, a signal box was provided on the line for the first time, located on the east side of the junction. Details of its design are not recorded although it was known to contain a frame of 14 levers. It was probably of timber construction; provided at the expense of the SMA the work was carried out by the GWR and so it is likely the box and equipment were of standard design. A surviving sketch from the time of the Board of Trade inspection of 1882 affords an idea of the equipment provided although this would appear to be at variance with the 1881 agreement over the actual junction. A 10 mph speed restriction applied to all movements at the junction, which was just under 500 yards from Marlborough station.

From the sketch it can be seen that besides the obvious junction signals, further signals were provided to control trains entering and leaving the terminus. It is likely these were operated from the junction signal box although not the turnouts at the terminus, which were beyond the limit for accepted mechanical control.

As has been referred to in the text, it was not until 1883 that through trains commenced running from the SMA via the new junction and thence to Savernake and Andover. Coinciding with this was the introduction of 'staff and ticket' working betwen Savernake West and Marlborough South Junction with the following arrangements in use for the sections.

Savernake West - Marlborough South Junction:
Triangular staff - colour yellow

Marlborough South Junction - Marlborough Station:
Round staff - colour white
'Tickets' corresponded with the colour of the appropriate train staff.

An official record dated 1st June 1892 refers to the provision of a ground level signal cabin at Marlborough, which was subsequently erected on the station platform at the west end of the main building. Constructed partly of timber with brick used for the sides and rear, it contained a 15 lever frame; floor dimensions were 18ft 6ins x 9ft 6ins. The estimated cost of the signal box together with equipment was put at £615 athough the actual cost was less then this and in 1894 was stated to have been £529.0s.1d. The figures included the '.. necessary signals as well as throw off points and a re-arrangement of the locking in the existing cabin' - referring to the South Junction. It may be taken then that by now interlocking was certainly provided at the terminus, although in all probability a start had been made on this consequent upon the provision of the Junction signal box in 1882 which by implication would appear to have had a conventional interocking frame. Although the actual date of commissioning of the new station signal box is not reported, it may well have been slightly earlier than the middle of the year, for on 8th February 1892 an order was placed with the signal works at Reading for a cast nameplate, 'Marlborough Signal Box'. Around this time large numbers of cast signal box plates were being ordered for locations throughout the GWR system, although an order for a plate for the South Junction box is noticable by its absence.*

The arrangements for working between the two signal boxes at Marlborough are not reported at this time although the following year (1893) Webb-Thompson electric train staff working was introduced on the branch in two separate sections, Savernake West to Marlborough South Junction, and Marlborough South Junction to Marlborough Station.

Supervision of both signal boxes at Marlborough was exercised by the local station master. Marlborough South Junction signal box was closed following the abolition of the connection between the two systems in June 1898 and the electric train staff working confined to a single staff section from Savernake West to Marlborough. The former double junction and signals were removed although the actual signal box structure, it is believed, was not removed until 1905, when it was reportedly sold. The intervening years may have seen its use as a store hut or office.

Little affected the signalling at Marlborough for the remainder of the line's existence, although a suggestion has been made that the former 'point discs' were superseded by 'independent discs' at some stage. Catch points had been provided since at least 1892.

With the reinstatement of the connection between the GWR and former M&SWJ routes in 1926 a ground frame was provided on the Marlborough branch, locked by the train staff.

A view of the yard, around harvest time judging by the number of open wagons with tarpaulins. There is also apparently a tar boiler possibly being used in connection with road works in the district.

L.G.R.P

The station box was closed from 15th February 1933, the signals removed and all points at the High Level station converted to hand operation. Coinciding with this a new signal box was opened at Marlborough Low Level in which levers 16 and 17 - respectively the independent disc and catchpoint, controlled the exit from the High Level yard onto the up M&SWJ line. The locking of the ground frame on the former branch was also no longer dependent upon the train staff.

The opening times of the station signal box varied over the years according to the requirements of the timetable, quoted in 1900 as 'open for the day's service' and closed from 9 pm Saturdays to 6 am Monday. An adjustment was obviously made during the periods when a Sunday service was in operation. This was simplified in 1920 to a brief heading 'closed after days train service'.

Despite being ordered by the local district signalling inspector direct to the GWR signal works at Reading, the cast signal box nameplates were produced within the Swindon works foundry.

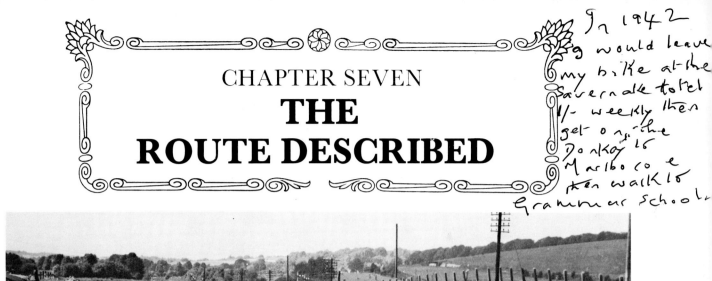

In 1942 g would leave my bike at the Savernake totel 1/- weekly then get on the Donkay to Marlboco e then walk to Grammar School.

→ Train nicknamed 'The Donkay'

Savernake looking west with a train, in the branch bay, preparing to leave for Marlborough Low Level.

Trains for Marlborough began their journey from a short bay at the west end of Savernake (Low Level) up platform. Part of this platform ran directly above the Kennet & Avon Canal Tunnel, passing underneath almost the whole of the station. The Marlborough bay had no run round loop and so after arrival the engine would back the empty stock out onto the branch loop before running round and then propelling the coaches into the bay ready for the next journey. Auto working was not used.

The branch proper was encountered immediately upon leaving the bay, the fireman collecting the train staff from the signalman at the west signal box as the train traversed the 16 chain radius curve from the bay. Turning away from the West of England main line in a north westerly direction for the first part of the journey at least the route is level, continuing over a short length of double track and past the down advanced starting signal which allowed access onto the single track section. There were no intermediate signal boxes or crossing places between Savernake and Marlborough.

To the right is a shallow cutting, whilst on the left is a refuge siding for the main line, followed by open fields ending in a drop to the canal. Beyond this is the main line. As the cutting side falls away to the right, it is possible to glimpse for the first time the neighbouring M & SWJ route, the two lines appearing slowly to converge. Before this however the branch begins to swing to the

left via a 40ch. curve, at the same time commencing a climb. The contours of Savernake Forest and the Marlborough Downs dictate that the branch climbs no less than 142 feet in just 3¾ miles. It is easy to appreciate the observations of the M&SWJ company, concerning the difficulties of working their trains over the line back in the 1880s.

At the end of the curve there is a shallow cutting before passing over a gated occupation crossing. The M&SWJ is now very close and separated only by a matter of a few yards of open field. Both lines part again as we pass the distant signal warning up trains of the approach to Savernake.

Just before the 71 mile post from Paddington, the line crosses the parish boundary separating Burbage parish from Savernake Great Park; most of the land in the area was once in the ownership of the Marquis of Ailesbury. To left and right there are the remains of some abandoned chalk workings though it is not known if these had any railway significance.

The line is now on an embankment increasing in height as the main Salisbury - Marlborough road appears on the left. The road is visibly climbing, its distance from the railway reduced until it passes underneath at Leigh Hill bridge. The gap to be spanned was only 29 feet but the resultant bridge was set at the skew angle of 57½ degrees to the road. Immediately after the bridge, and alongside the road is a stone cottage appropriately named Leigh Hill Lodge, which from its appearance may well

SAVERNAKE

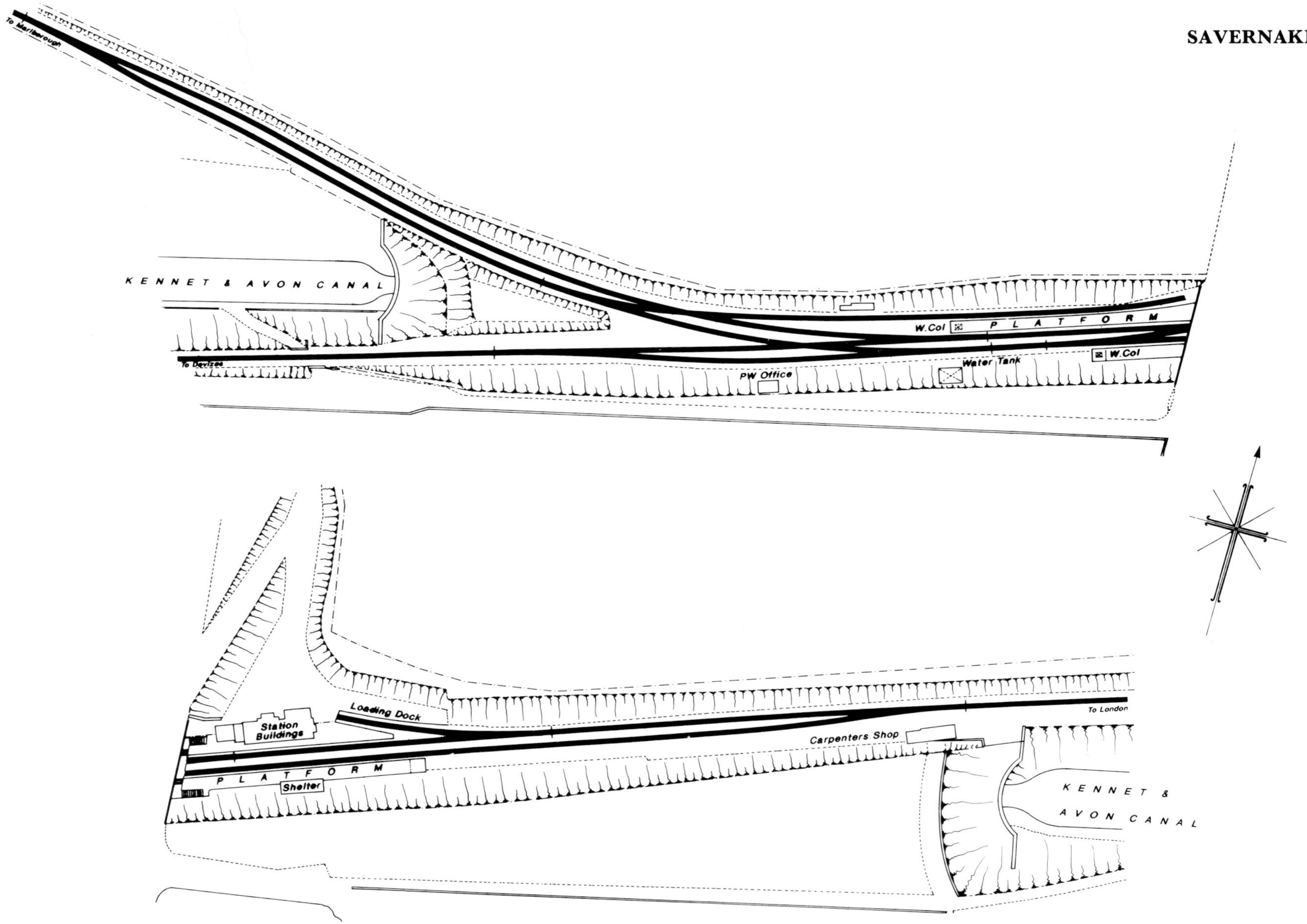

KENNET & AVON CANAL

PLATFORM

W.Col

W.Col

Water Tank

PW Office

To Marlborough

To Devizes

KENNET & AVON CANAL

To London

Carpenters Shop

Loading Dock

Station Buildings

PLATFORM

Shelter

KENNET & AVON CANAL

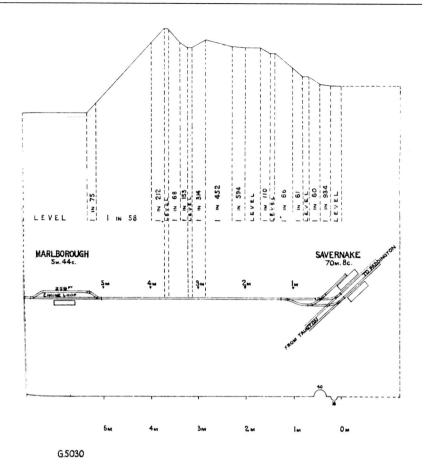

G.5030

With the closing of a section of the original Marlborough Branch in 1933 (see Chapter 8) the GWR and later BR, maintained a shuttle service between Savernake Low Level and Marlborough, although this now started from the latter Low Level station. As far as Savernake was concerned the service was little altered from that which had existed in previous years and it is seen here in BR days in the charge of an unidentified 55xx, at the head of two coaches and a van waiting to leave for Marlborough.

Lens of Sutton

have been a toll house many years earlier.

On both sides now are clumps of deciduous trees through which, on the right, the bridge carrying the M&SWJ line over the same road can be seen, a short distance away. As the embankment subsides both lines can be seen moving closer together again, after which there is another occupation crossing before entering the cutting, a ¼ mile long, which ends with a slight curve to the right. At the end of the cutting the ground is level for a moment before falling away sharply to allow the Wootton Rivers - Marlborough road to pass underneath at right angles. The M&SWJ line crosses the same road a few yards north with both lines now at their closest point. The original road was diverted at the time the Marlborough railway was built, although it is still possible to see the stub ends running at an acute angle to terminate alongside the railway. A few yards further on in 1933 the original branch was slewed to join the former M&SWJ, the actual point of divergence of the Marlborough Branch taking it through another shallow cutting.

To the left is the area known as Clench Common; unfortunately invisible from the train on the same side are distant views of Salisbury plain, although as the cutting eases and is replaced by a low embankment it may just be possible to catch a glimpse of the Pewsey White Horse. Much of the countryside adjacent to the Marlborough Branch is rightly renowned for its turf monuments and relics of Ancient Britain.

This particular section of the line skirts the fringes of the ancient forest and is probably the most picturesque point on the branch. In summer an abundance of wild poppies grow alongside the line whilst nearby there is the lush greenery of both meadowland and pasture.*

The M&SWJ line is now moving away to the right and we will soon lose sight of it completely as the branch pases Park Farm to the right. Just past the 72¼ mile post there is another gated occupation crossing, the railway now straight and level

for a short distance before resuming its upward climb. The shallow embankment resumes with a 2 ft culvert underneath, after which there is yet another cutting. Perhaps surprisingly, despite the number of crossings on the route no accidents involving any of these are recorded throughout the railway's lifetime.

The cutting continues for almost a quarter of a mile and is followed by a short sharp embankment in the midst of which is a brick arch affording road access to Tarrents Farm. We are now approximately mid way with the railway still climbing but this time on the shallower gradient of 1 in 452. The route gently alternates between cutting and embankment and soon passes two or more minor crossings; there is a small permanent way hut on the right followed by another embankment and cutting. Apart from the station limits this is the only confirmed site for a p.w. hut anywhere on the branch and the location of other huts associated with the 1910 'economic system of maintenance' are not shown on official plans. As the cutting gradually comes to an end there is a short section where the railway follows the height of the land - for much of the time curving gently right around the fringe of the forest.

Just by the 73½ mile post the cutting resumes in the middle of which comes a mellow brick overbridge known as Rowberry Arch, carrying a narrow occupation road to Levitts Farm which stands on the south side of the railway. Close to the cutting's end there is yet another occupation crossing after which the route turns sharp right onto an embankment. In the midst of this another culvert passes beneath, the railway now approaching the 74 mile post from Paddington and the top of its

* *The 1908 GWR guide book 'Wonderful Wessex' refers briefly to the origins of the name Savernake Forest. Said to come from the reference Safernoc, in use in 93 AD, the name derived from the words 'saverne' - a sweet fern and 'acre' - the equivalent for land.*

The Marlborough branch crossing of the A345 main road at Leigh Hall, Savernake Forest, viewed towards Marlborough. The bridge parapet forms a gentle and symetrical curve but the apparent dip at the end is an illusion of the photograph. The bridge here was 29ft long at a skew to the road of 57½ degrees. In the background is the bridge carrying the Marlborough and Grafton line over the same road, with the early sign between the two worthy of a second glance.

T.B. Sands

A superb study of a 55xx tank heading a three coach train between Marlborough and Savernake, on the course of the original route. Taken in early BR days the engine and stock nevertheless still display the evidence of private ownership. The clarity of the print has allowed the coaches to be identified; left to right are a former 'Toplight' Brake 3rd of 1908 rebuilt to Diagram D56, a Corridor 3rd either to Diagram C64 or C65 of 1933 and a Brake Composite to Diagram E153 and Lot 1572 of 1936.

J.F. Russell Smith

The Marlborough and Grafton railway ran parallel with the original branch for some distance near Savernake and although originally built with double track one line was lifted over part of its route following the rationalisation of 1933. This lovely study shows an SR Mogul, No. 31626, with a three coach train between Savernake and Marlborough, running on the remaining single track of the former Marlborough and Grafton line.

J.F. Russell Smith

MARLBOROUGH

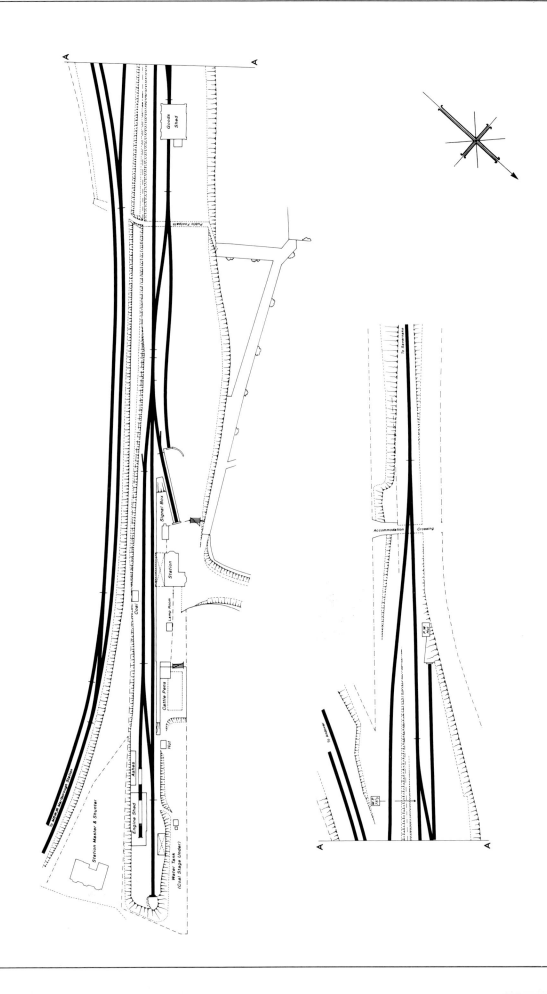

climb from Savernake. The summit itself is marked by a brief section of level track after which comes the descent to the terminus, including over a mile at 1 in 58. Bearing in mind the 1888 proposal for a passng loop on the branch it is interesting to speculate where this might in fact have been located.

The various timetables contained in previous chapters show the normal running time for trains over the branch being 12-15 minutes. Goods and mixed trains would of necessity take several minutes longer for they would pause at the summit to pin down sufficient brakes on the freight vehicles before commencing the steep descent to either Marlborough or Savernake. Fixed warning boards informing drivers of this requirement stood near this point for down trains and close to the Savernake branch distant signal for up trains.

The descent commences then with the railway and ground level together, although this does not last long; the line soon plunges into another cutting with a single brick arch overhead. This bridge carries an occupation road to Wernham Farm, again on the south side of the railway. All the bridges both over and under the branch were built for just a single track. This particular cutting is both the longest and deepest on the whole ralway and the line, still curving right slightly is by now travelling almost due north.

At the end of the cutting the railway is once more on what appears to be level ground even if in fact it is still descending. There now begins the high embankment which caused some settling difficulties when the line was new, whilst from its vantage point the Marlborough - Pewsey road can be seen running alongside, the actual area referred to as Preshute. A brick arch carries the railway over another minor road and footpath, leading to Greatham Farm some distance away on the east side of the railway.

To the right, but invisible as yet is the M&SWJ line, the two routes slowly coming together with the original branch now following an almost dead straight course for the remainder of its route. Some few hundred yards away to the right is the site of the ancient village of Pantawick, now recognised merely by a series of depressions in the earth.

As the embankment comes to an end the down distant signal for Marlborough is passed on the left after which comes the last of the occupation crossings. There is then another brief cutting and then another embankment which continues to the start of the station area. The terminus itself is on level ground and slightly raised above the surrounding area.

Travelling from Savernake the distance covered to Marlborough has been almost exactly 5½ miles with no intermediate stations. No plans have been found to suggest there was ever any consideration given to the provision of an intermediate halt. The sparsely populated forest was unlikely to have rewarded such a provision.

Approaching the station itself the driver would sound one note on the engine whistle, the officially recognised code for an arriving train. When shunting was taking place however there could at times be a cacophony of sound when entering or leaving the loop, three long blasts for the goods shed and no less than four separate notes for the horse box siding - it is surprising the latter was not considered as invalid for fear of frightening the unfortunate beasts!

Beyond the station the railway continues for a short distance before terminating at a set of buffer stops beyond which there is a steep drop to the main road through Savernake Forest. The M&SWJ station, Marlborough Low Level, stands a short distance away on the opposite side of the road.

A fortunate find in the GWR Magazine of 1916 - ....*the removal of the last section of longitudinal road in the running line at Marlborough.....*The implication then is that the trackwork had remained unaltered since the alteration of the gauge in 1874! The photograph also provides a clear view of the signal box front and the station canopy which reveals it had no skylights. The canopy survived until about 1947. The signal box at the station had a floor area of 18'6" x 9'6" and contained a 15 lever frame. It was not provided with a closing switch. Signal maintenance was under the control of the Savernake signal lineman and who besides covering the branch also maintained the main line from Hampstead Crossing (between Newbury and Kintbury) to Woodborough.

GWR Magazine

The aftermath of the head-on collision at Marlborough on 17th February 1900, when an engine and snow plough struck an engine stabled in the shed. Although it is not possible to positively identify the locomotives involved it is possible that the one on the right may be a member of the 0-6-0 'Standard Goods' class.

Swindon Society

Seen from the rear of the shed the stationary occupant has been pushed backwards some distance as a result of the collision, although again it is impossible to positively identify it. In the background the branch tank engine is standing at the far end of the run-round loop.

Swindon Society

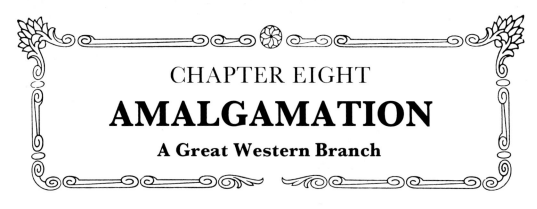

CHAPTER EIGHT
AMALGAMATION
A Great Western Branch

The change of ownership of 1896 had little if any outward effect upon the operation of the former Marlborough Railway, for as will be recalled, the branch had been worked from its inception by the GWR. Change came two years later, from June 1898, when M&SWJ traffic ceased consequent upon the opening of the Marlborough and Grafton line. At the same time the connection at Marlborough South Junction was abandoned.

From this time on the Marlborough Railway reverted to its original status as a branch line with competition for traffic between the stations at either end of the line, unlike the period 1864-1883.

Before the year 1898 had ended Savernake was the scene of a minor accident involving the branch train, reported briefly in the official minutes of the Locomotive Carriage and Wagon Departent Committee: *At Savernake on 31/10/1898 the 7.52 branch passenger train* (am or pm is not specified) *from Marlborough came into contact with a truck that was standing against the stop-block. The driver states he applied the brake at the distant signal as usual, but that, owing to the rails being covered with leaves the brake would not act.* There is no record of injury or damage and no information as to the engine involved or possible outcome of the inquiry.

Two years later on 17th February 1900 another incident occurred, this time at Marlborough station. On this occasion official comment is surprisingly missing, *The Marlborough Times* providing the only clue as to the actual event.

It would appear that parts of Wiltshire, including the branch, were at that time adversely affected by a sudden and severe snow fall. Consequent upon this Swindon despatched a tender engine to assist the normal tank on the branch, which at the end of the day stabled in the shed at Marlborough. The engine was positioned by the stop blocks at the end of the platform. A further severe snowfall then occurred prompting the Marlborough station master to request a snow plough from Swindon. This duly arrived though the engine and plough got out of control on the steep descent to the terminus and collided head on with the tender engine waiting in the shed. The force of the collision was sufficient to push the stationary locomotive back some 30 feet through the wooden end of the engine shed. There is no record of injury or the identities of the persons and machines involved.

The same year, 1900, finds the first reference to a special for Collegians to Marlborough although the implication is that this type of working had long been commonplace.

GWR Locomotive, Carriage and Wagon Department, Swindon
To T.J. Allen Esq.
29th September 1900
Dear Sir,
6.20 p.m. Paddington to Marlborough, 21st September with Collegians.

With reference to our previous correspondence on this subject, on all future occasions I shall be glad if you will arrange for this special to be worked as follows.

Paddington engine to work through to Savernake, tank goods engine to be sent from Trowbridge light to work special Savernake to Marlborough and taking empty stock back to Savernake.

Paddington engine to work empty stock back to Paddington engine to be turned at Reading.

When the special is run from Marlborough to Paddington the following arrangements should be made: Paddington engine to work empty stock to Savernake and sufficient time should be allowed at Reading for the engine to turn so as to run tender first Reading to Savernake. Two branch engines to work empty stock Savernake to Marlborough and the special back to Savernake. The Paddington engine to work special Savernake to Paddington.

I shall be glad if you will so arrange times as to allow the branch engines being free to do the work assisted by the spare engine which is lighted up for the purpose as if this is not done we have to send an engine from Trowbridge to work over the branch.

Please let me know that you will do what is necessary and at the same time perhaps you will kindly say if there is any reason why tender engines should not be allowed to work passenger trains over the Marlborough branch.

Yours truly,
Signed: W.H. Waister

Attached to the same file was a further brief note:
7th November 1900

With regard to the last paragraph of your letter of 29th September, I do not see that we can allow tender engines to work passenger trains over this branch in view of the Board of Trade regulations that the line should be worked by tank engines.

Although the year such special services commenced is not recorded what is clear is the importance placed upon such trains by the GWR. The report reveals a number of points concerning the working of the line; at times there were two engines at Marlborough and the shed seems to have worked as an outstation of Trowbridge. The reference to tank engines working the branch exclusively is in fact well known, for an entry to this effect is to be found in the GWR Sectional Appendix to the Working Timetable. A further official document explains that *the college* services should be double headed and although only goods loadings are quoted, a single engine was only allowed to take a maximum of 13 loaded wagons, equivalent to about 130 tons.

Moving ahead in time a few years it is known that by 1918 an arrangement was reached whereby one of the 36XX 2-4-2T class engines was utilised on the college trains, official correspondence recording the event as follows:

27th July and 10th August 1918
Specials with cadets, Marlborough - Paddington and return
Arranged with Mr. Crump for these trains to be worked by engines of the 36XX class so that it can work through to Marlborough and save lighting up the second branch engine and finding men from Trowbridge.

Engines of this type were at the time allocated to the London area on suburban trains whilst a solitary example was also shedded at Reading.

Despite the apparent extravagance of the two engines and therefore two sets of men to work one particular class of service, in other areas economy was very much the order of the day. Together with a number of other minor branches on the system the GWR instigated the 'economic system of maintenance' on the Marlborough branch, bringing it into use on 1st August 1910. This involved the substitution of one gang of six men for the two gangs of four which had previously been responsible for the track. Under the new arrangements the ganger in charge was provided with a self propelled rail trolley - in appearance not dissimilar to a bicycle attached to a side car, kept in motion by a push pull method on the handlebars. In theory then the ganger could easily inspect the railway between trains using his new transport although it is likely this involved quite an amount of muscle power on the steep gradients. He was however still expected to walk 'the length' at least once a week.

The remainder of the gang were also provided with a trolley, this time of the pump type. It could be used to transport men or materials to the site of work when required and to safeguard operations a system of 'occupation key' working was provided. This has previously been described in detail in a number of other publications but to briefly recap, a brass key was provided the release of which was electrically interlocked with the electric train staff in use on the line. Unlike the train staff however which could only be used from the signal boxes at Savernake West and Marlborough, a number of occupation key instruments were provided at intervals along the line, separating it into sections of suitable length.

A 'staff' for the driver of a train could only be obtained by the signalman (with of course the co-operaton of the man at the other end of the section) provided the ganger's occupation key was inserted in one of the special instruments provided. Likewise to release the occupation key the co-operation of both signalmen was needed and this could only take place if all the train staffs were restored in the instruments. The ganger was also provided wth a 'portable telephone', contemporary records suggesting this was a heavy and cumbersome affair, which could be plugged in at various points mid section and with which the ganger could speak to the signalman at either end of the line. In this way minimum disruption was afforded to the train service whilst it was possible for one man to manoeuvre the inspection trolley off the rails, affording precedence to a train when required. Records state the cost of the installation though the fate of the two displaced men is not reported:

Telephones and occupation key instruments for use in huts at Savernake
and Marlborough. £80.00.0
5 Telephone Huts £ 7.10.0
1 Velocipede Car Hut £ 3. 0.0
1 Velocipede Car £ 7.10.0
1 Mechanical Trolley £11.5.01 *Watch* £ 2. 0.0
1 Suit oilskins for ganger 15/-.

Under standard rule branch maintained by 2 gangs of 4 men.
    Wages p/a   *Men/mile*
    £396.10.0   1.38

Under new system only one gang of 6 men:

    Wages p/a   *Men/mile*
    £287.06.0   1.04

Gross saving of 2 men and £109.04.0d p/a.

This method of maintaining the line remained in operation until the branch closed.

The Country Bus Services

In addition to the local train service between Savernake and Marlborough the GWR selected the latter location as a centre for the development of 'road motor' buses intended to supplement the rail network and so provide a 'feeder' service to the trains.

At this point it is worth mentioning that the GWR was one of the pioneers of the railway motor-bus within the United Kingdom and the first of the main line railway companies of England to begin such a service.* This commenced in August 1903 in Cornwall, from Helston to the Lizard, followed by a number of other services so that by the start of October 1904 a total of 22 routes were operating.

From 10th October 1904 a service commenced between Marlborough and Calne although this was in effect the second public omnibus between the two towns; a horse-bus had run from the opening of the Marlborough branch in 1864 though how long it remained in operation is not certain. Another, undated, proposal concerns a plan to link the two towns by means of a light railway; estimated to cost £75,000 this was not proceeded with. (It is possible that the bus service was instigated to test public response for a railway).

The GWR Marlborough to Calne road motor service commenced from the station yard at Marlborough and ran via a number of villages, the most important of which was Avebury - well known for its pre-historic stones and earthworks. Three trips were made each way on weekdays only initially using a Milnes - Daimler vehicle. The timetable referred to the service calling at 'halts' at the various villages. Out of hours the bus was stabled at Marlborough station.

The next service came some five years later, when on 2nd October 1909 a thrice-weekly service commenced between Marlborough, Ramsbury and Hungerford. 'Dennis' vehicles were used with Swindon built bodies. This service was however, short lived in its original form, terminating less than two years later on 30th September 1911. Just three days later on 3rd October 1911 a replacement service commenced, from Marlborough or Hungerford to Ramsbury and Aldbourne varying according to the day of the week - possibly in connection with the various market days. It would appear that on certain occasions the service was extended through to Swindon.

With effect from 15th July 1912, this hotchpotch of routes was crystalized into a twice weekly service between Marlborough, Ramsbury, Aldbourne and Swindon, though again the arrangements were short lived. It was quickly apparent that the buses could not achieve a viable financial return and at the end of September 1913 all were withdrawn, including the original Calne service. Marlborough thus ceased operation as a GWR bus centre although not it would appear without an amount of criticism, for the loss of the Calne service was particulary mourned and became the subject of complaint in the local press.

But this was destined not to be the end of the GWR as a bus operator in the area; on 24th July 1924 the Marlborough depot was re-opened and services restored to Ramsbury and Hungerford and also to Calne. The latter was one of the first to be operated by a Chevrolet 22 hp motor bus although this was replaced the following year, 1925, by a Thornycroft 'A1' vehicle equipped for one man operation. The reason for the change of heart is thought to have been to forestall encroachment into GWR territory by the Bristol Tramway Company, then rapidly expanding their own network.

* The Belfast & Northern Counties Railway and Northern Counties Committee had commenced a service between Whiteabbey and Greenisland in April 1902 whilst the narrow gauge Lynton and Barnstaple ran a road motor service between Ilfracombe and Blackmoor Station for some two months from 30th May 1903. The North Eastern Railway was the second main line company in England to institute a road motor service, between Beverley and Beeford from 7th September 1903.

A delightful picture of the GWR road motor service that operated between Marlborough and Calne, outside Marlborough station. The vehicle, No. AF 64, was a 'Milnes-Daimler' 20 hp, first registered on 3rd February 1904. Fleet No. 5 was carried. The solid rubber tyres, open top and exposed staircase are obvious features but notice also the wooden destination board proclaiming 'Marlborough - Calne'; on the reverse side it advertised the route in the opposite direction. Between the rear of the bus and signal box it is possible to glimpse part of a 'syphon' van possibly being used for the carriage of milk churns. The horse drawn goods vehicle is standing on the roadway leading to the goods yard whilst behind is another horse drawn vehicle; it may well be a horse bus, though it would not be operated by the GWR. The photograph would appear to have been taken post-1908.

AF 64 again, this time leaving *The Red Lion* at Avebury on the Marlborough to Calne service. In the background it is possible to discern a number of poster boards, which held timetable and advertising information on the service.

G.W.R. ROAD·MOTOR SERVICES.

In connection with the Company's Trains, Road Motor Cars are run between the places mentioned below :—

MARLBOROUGH AND CALNE.

Passing through Manton, Fyfield, Overton, West Kennet, Avebury, Beckhampton, Yatesbury, Cherhill, and Quemerford.

WEEK DAYS ONLY.

FARES

Between	And Marlboro'.	Manton.	Fyfield.	Overton.	West Kennet.	Avebury.	Beck-hampton.	Yatesbury.	Cherhill.	Quemer-ford.	Calne.
	s. d.	s. d.	s. d.	s. d.	s. d.	s. d.	s. d.	s. d.	s. d.	s. d.	s. d.
MARLBOROUGH Railway Station or "The Ailesbury Arms Hotel"	...	0 2	0 4	0 6	0 8	0 10	0 10	1 0	1 2	1 4	1 6
MANTON	0 2	...	0 2	0 4	0 6	0 8	0 8	0 10	1 0	1 2	1 4
FYFIELD	0 4	0 2	...	0 2	0 4	0 6	0 6	0 8	0 10	1 0	1 2
OVERTON	0 6	0 4	0 2	...	0 2	0 4	0 4	0 6	0 8	0 10	1 0
WEST KENNET	0 8	0 6	0 4	0 2	...	0 2	0 4	0 6	0 8	0 10	0 10
AVEBURY	0 10	0 8	0 6	0 4	0 2	...	0 2	0 4	0 6	0 8	0 10
BECKHAMPTON Cross Roads	0 10	0 8	0 6	0 4	0 4	0 2	...	0 2	0 4	0 6	0 6
YATESBURY Cross Roads	1 0	0 10	0 8	0 6	0 6	0 4	0 2	...	0 2	0 4	0 4
CHERHILL	1 2	1 0	0 10	0 8	0 8	0 6	0 4	0 2	...	0 4	0 4
QUEMERFORD	1 4	1 2	1 0	0 10	0 10	0 8	0 6	0 4	0 4	...	0 2
CALNE Railway Station	1 6	1 4	1 2	1 0	0 10	0 10	0 8	0 6	0 4	0 2	...

CHEAP RETURN TICKETS, available on the day of issue only, will be issued to Marlborough on Mondays and Saturdays and to Calne on Saturdays, at the undermentioned fares :—

To MARLBOROUGH—Mondays and Saturdays.

From AVEBURY - - 1s.
 ,, OVERTON - - 8d.
 ,, FYFIELD - - 6d.

To CALNE—Saturdays only.

From Cherhill - - 6d.
 ,, Quemerford - 3d.

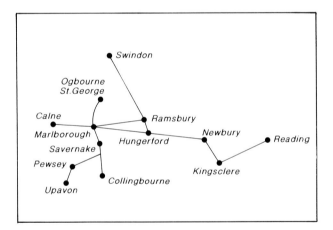

Another 20 hp Milnes-Daimler, AM 487, near *The Red Lion* **at Avebury. Two vehicles were used on the service with, it would appear, slight modifications - notice the steps leading to the roof top luggage area.**

Lens of Sutton

On 14th August 1925 another new service commenced from Marlborough to Collingbourne Ducis via Savernake (Low Level) station. The original intention had been for this bus to continue to Ludgershall but for an unreported reason this did not take place. Again this was another unsuccessful venture and only lasted until 6th November in the same year. Why such a service should have commenced at all in direct competition to the former M&SWJ and now GWR line is inexplicable.

The GWR's involvement with road motor bus operation in many ways mirrored its behaviour with regard to small railway companies; during 1927 it took over the business of a Mr. Page from Ramsbury who had been operating a single 14-seat Ford bus on the Marlborough to Hungerford route. Later in the same year 'through' bus services commenced between Calne, Marlborough and Hungerford, later extended east as far as Reading via Newbury and Kingsclere.

From 14th November 1928 there was also a service from Marlborough north to the village of Ogbourne St.George. As with the majority of the bus routes this probably ran either weekdays only or on alternate weekdays, with no Sunday runs.

A further service commenced on 1st May 1929 between Marlborough (Low Level) station and Upavon, the route taking in Savernake (Low Level) station and Pewsey. In its original form this was short lived and was soon cut back to Pewsey although GWR attempts to successfully operate what was in effect three separate and competing public passenger services between Marlborough and Savernake must appear strange. On the same day in May 1929 a service commenced between the former M&SWJ station at Marlborough, now the 'Low Level' station, and the High Street of the town. At the same time a GWR booking and receiving office was also established in the High Street, for which the railway paid an annual rental of £60.

Either BH7 or BH269 at Avebury, this time in what appears to be overall brown livery. The person boarding the vehicle is Mr B.Hiller.

The services had now reached a zenith, which included on the periphery buses to a number of neighbouring villages, originating from the GWR stations at Lambourn and Swindon. In addition there were 'land cruises' to the town and downland nearby. The peak though was to be short-lived, for as early as 1st April 1930 curtailment commenced with the Marlborough to Ogbourne St.George service. The remainder of the routes - which by now operated out of the Low Level station, only lasted until 8th February 1932 when all were handed over to Bristol Tramways, including the separate routes to Calne, Hungerford and Pewsey.

From this point the Bristol Tramways buses did not call at either of the Marlborough stations and instead began in the town itself. The bus company stabled four of their vehicles in the yard of Messrs G. Cope & Co. Coal Merchants.

Having dwelt upon the internal combustion engine it is time once again to return to rail transport and the impact of the First World War upon the little branch.

Unlike its neighbour, the M&SWJ, the original Marlborough branch did not play a major role in the movement of wartime supplies, though it is known that fodder and timber traffic increased, much of it loaded in the yard at Marlborough and destined for the military depots at Ludgershall and Tidworth. Throughout the GWR system there was a great reduction in staffing levels as men voluteered for military service which was offset wherever possible by the employment of women in the clerical and labouring grades.

The final years of the branch commenced with the passing of the 1921 Railways Act; in 1923 this brought about the absorption of the former M&SWJ system into the GWR, and a change of emphasis. The competition between the two companies for Marlborough - Savernake traffic was now effectively at an end and was instead now seen as an undesirable duplication of route and resources. Not surprisingly, it did not take long for change to come about; it began in a small way with the separate identification of the stations under the term 'Low

MARLBOROUGH & SAVERNAKE LOW LEVEL STATION

	WEEK DAYS										SUNDAYS.	
	a.m.	a.m.	a.m.	p.m.	p.m.	p.m.	p.m.	p.m.	p.m.	p.m.	p.m.	
MARLBOROUGH (G.W.R. Office) dp	7 46	8 57	10 50	12 28	2 3	5 47	7 11	7 59	6 8	..
(Stn. Approach) „	7 49	9B0	10 53	12 31	2 6	5 50	7 14	8 2	6 11	..
CADLEY .. .. „	7 54	9 5	10 58	12 36	2 11	5 55	7 19	8 7	6 16	..
SAVERNAKE (Low Level Stn.) arr.	8 6	9 17	11 10	12 48	2 23	6 7	7 31	8 19	6 28	..
SAVERNAKE (L.L. Stn.) .. de.	8 11	8 25	9 22	9 33	11 15	12 53	1 0	2 28	6 15	7 36	7 50	8 24	6 33	..
DEVIZES .. .. arr.	..	9 20	..	10 5	11 47	1 25	..	3 20	..	..	8 22	..	..	..
HUNGERFORD .. .. „	8 27	..	9 33	..	..	..	1 14	..	6 31	To Pease. Westbury. West-mouth.	..	8 44	7N11	..
NEWBURY .. .. „	8 43	..	9 48	..	..	..	1 32	..	6 46	..	9 8	7N28	..
READING .. .. „	9 12	..	10C13	..	..	..	2 3	..	7 23	..	9 47	8 14	..
PADDINGTON .. .. „	10 0	..	10 50	..	..	..	2 55	..	8 10	..	10 55	7 55	..

	WEEK DAYS.										SUNDAYS.	
	a.m.	a.m.	a.m.	a.m.	a.m.	p.m.	p.m.	p.m.	p.m.	p.m.	p.m.	
PADDINGTON .. .. dep.	..	7 15	..	8 40	10 45	..	12 30	3 20	..	..	K	..
READING .. .. „	..	8 28	..	9 30	11 42	..	1 17	4 38	..	..	..	..
NEWBURY .. .. „	..	8 57	..	10 40	12 25	..	1 52	5 17	7 18	..	..	..
HUNGERFORD .. .. „	..	9 14	..	10 57	12 40	..	2 9	5 35	7 34	..	..	..
DEVIZES .. .. „	8 46	..	9 38	..	..	12 25	..	..	7 36	..	6 12	..
SAVERNAKE (L.L. Stn.) .. arr.	9 20	9 31	10 28	11 13	12 55	12 58	2 27	5 52	7 49	8 20	6 52	..
SAVERNAKE (Low Level Stn.) dep.	9 25	9 36	11 18	..	1 3	2 32	6 10	8 25	..	..	6 56	..
CADLEY .. .. „	9 37	9 48	11 30	..	1 15	2 44	6 22	8 37	..	..	7 8	..
MARLBOROUGH (Stn. Approach) „	9B42	9 53	11 35	..	1 20	2 49	6 27	8 42	..	..	7 13	..
(G.W.R. Office) arr.	9 45	9 56	11 38	..	1 23	2 52	6 30	8 45	..	..	7 16	..

B—Low Level Station.   C—By Slip Coach.   K—Connection from Bristol (Temple Meads) 3.25 p.m., Bath 3.55 p.m., Westbury 6.6 p.m. and West of England.   N—Savernake (L.L.) Station depart 6.55 p.m.

ROAD TRANSPORT DEPARTMENT.

New Omnibus Service.—Hungerford and Marlborough.—On May 1st the Company inaugurated a new omnibus service between Marlborough and Hungerford. The principal feature of the new service is the linking up at Hungerford with the rail, and speedier and additional up-line connections. An omnibus leaves the receiving office that the Company has set up at No. 9, High Street, Marlborough, at 7.48 a.m. for Hungerford, enabling Paddington to be reached at 10 a.m., nearly half an hour saving in time. A new London connection is given by omnibus leaving the High Street at 10.50 a.m. for Hungerford, enabling Paddington to be reached at 12.55 p.m.

From Hungerford a new connection is given off the 9.15 a.m. ex Paddington, arriving at Marlborough High Street at 12.10 p.m., and services are run off the 2.45 and 6 p.m. ex Paddington, reaching Marlborough at 4.48 and 7.54 p.m., respectively. On Wednesdays and Saturdays a later connection from London is given off the 7.55 p.m. ex Paddington. A new bus service runs between Marlborough and Savernake, extended in certain cases to Burbage, Easton, Milton, Pewsey, and Upavon. New services have been introduced on the Hungerford, Ramsbury, Marlborough, Avebury, and Calne route, giving additional facilities for reaching Chippenham, Bath, and Bristol.

Level' and 'High Level' followed by a rationalisation of senior staff at both Marlborough and Savernake. Full details of these changes are given in the appropriate station chapters.

Meanwhile at Paddington discussion was taking place over the potential future of the Marlborough - Savernake lines resulting in a proposal to the Traffic Committee at its meeting of Thursday 21st May 1925:

Since the taking over the M&SW line consideration has been given to the possibility of providing a junction in the vicinity of Savernake between it and the GW Marlborough Branch to enable the latter to be closed, and certain economies to be effected. Such a junction can be put in at Savernake and it is recommended that this be done.

It will be necessary to provide a junction between the M&SW line and the GW branch at Marlborough for the convenient handling of goods traffic. The estimates are:-

Junction at Savernake
Junction at Marlborough
Engineer £3,250
Engineer £510
Signals £1,345
Signals £250
Land £200

Total 4,795 Total 760

Total £5,565

Economies estimated at £789 per annum will be possible, equal to 14.18% on the outlay.

It is worthwhile pausing for a moment to consider the implication of the figures quoted, which may also require a brief word of explanation. The reason for the difference in costings for the junction at Marlborough compared with that proposed at Savernake is simply explained, in that at Marlborough the formation of the original 1883 connection would be re-used (it can be assumed to still be in railway ownership). At Savernake however and despite the close proximity of the two systems near to Hat Gate, additional work and land purchase would be required. On the basis of the quoted figures a return on

investment would have been possible after just over seven years.

For reasons not explained the Savernake connection was not at this time proceeded with despite the following Minute: 'The proposals were approved and it was agreed to recommend the GWR Board to sanction the same.' Instead the connection between the two routes at Marlbrough was restored on the same site as years earlier, albeit in much simpler form than had existed between 1883 and 1898. Now there was just a single facing point from the original Marlborough branch which trailed onto the up line of the M&SWJ route. The puzzle though is what might this new connection have been used for at that time? Despite much thought and discussion the answer would appear to be precious little, for there was now no need for vehicle transfers between the two concerns, whilst the passenger services still continued to operate independently on the two lines as before.

It appeared then that the immediate future of the branch was secure, a view reinforced by a Minute of the GWR Traffic Department meeting of 25th April 1929:

'..the General Manager stated that in view of the representations which have been made by local interests it is now proposed to keep open the Marlborough Branch ..'

Just four years later however it was a different story, for with receipts falling there could now be little justification for retaining both lines. Accordingly on 6th March 1933 the engineers moved in and began a series of changes affecting the area, the most obvious being the closure of Marlborough High Level to passenger services. The station and branch had lasted slightly less than 70 years.

At the same time as the passenger closure, a new connection was instigated near to Hat Gate, Savernake in the same location as had been proposed in 1925. The former Marlborough branch line slewed across to join with the former up line of the M&SWJ. At Marlborough, stop blocks were erected on the old branch at a point 462 yards the Savernake side of the reinstated 1926 connection which still enabled trains to reach the former Marlborough High Level station, albeit with a reversal. The remaining portion of the original branch was abandoned and lifted soon afterwards.

At Savernake too there were changes, the former High Level station now having its track and signalling rationalised so as to provide a single line with passing loop for goods traffic, controlled by a series of ground frames. The former double line Marlborough and Grafton route was now in effect two parallel single tracks with the down line allowing trains to run via Savernake High Level and the up line taking trains to Savernake Low Level. Concurrent with this a number of signal alterations were effected at Marlborough as well as at the junctions at Wolfhall and Grafton South.

Marlborough High Level was now relegated in status to a goods station, its signal box closed and the various points converted to hand operation. In this guise it remained in use for a further thirty years and although not officially closed to goods until 7th September 1964 a run down took place long before that date. Supervision was exercised by the Marlborough Low Level station master. In the ensuing years there was a slow change of emphasis away from the railway as a carrier to that of the road lorry and accordingly receipts failed to equal rising operating costs. It came as no real surprise then to see the former station fall into disrepair, its buildings decaying whilst grass sprouted between tracks once so assiduously looked after by the ganger.

Elsewhere too there were difficulties. At Savernake falling receipts had led to the closure of the former High Level station to passengers from 15th September 1958; coinciding with this the staton master grade was withdrawn from Savernake Low Level where a Grade 1 porter was now in charge. The fatal blow

The effects of decay at Marlborough in 1947 and 14 years after passenger services ceased. The site survived as a goods depot for a further 17 years although becoming more desolate as time passed

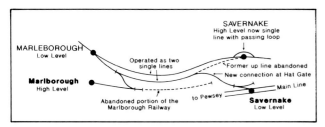

came in 1961, when from 11th September the Western Region withdrew passenger services from the former M&SWJ route. Fewer passengers than ever used Savernake Low Level station and consequently from 8th November 1965 it was relegated to 'unstaffed halt', goods traffic having previously been withdrawn from 19th May 1964. Closure eventually occured to all traffic on 18th April 1966 athough the station was survived by the East and West signal boxes; the latter the last to close, from 19th November 1978. The main line now comes under the control of the panel boxes at Westbury and Reading.

With the station long demolished, today's passenger travelling over the former Berks and Hants Extension route at Savernake in air-conditioned HST trains could be forgiven for not realising there had ever been a stopping place at that point. In Marlborough too the railway has long vanished, giving way to housing, whilst much of the trackbed has long reverted to its original use, farmland.

It is now fast approaching 130 years since the first serious proposals for a line to Marlborough were mooted and nearly 60 years since the last passenger train left the High Level station for Savernake. But for the intransigence of the GWR so many years earlier perhaps the branch might have lasted just a little longer.

Soon after the 1933 re-modelling, with the disused portion of the Marlborough branch in the foreground and new connection to the Marlborough and Grafton line running left to right. The view is looking towards Savernake.

Savernake station in the 1930s, with a dozen or so people on the platform. The station is known to have been particularly busy on Sunday evenings when up to *250 passengers* **would change off a local service to await the arrival of a London train from Taunton.**

D. Thompson

CHAPTER NINE

WORKING THE LINE

From the earliest days train services reflected the nature of the line - a quiet rural backwater. This changed little over the years and as a result the public timetables might appear at first glance not to have altered much although, as will be seen later, this was often not quite the case.

In 1864 five trains each way are shown on the line - see Chapter 4 - a type of service which continued until at least 1875. Surprisingly a public timetable for June 1865 only reports three trains each way although it is possible this referred only to the *passenger* services and not the two mixed trains by then also operating. No Sunday service is shown.

In the July - December timetable of 1875 another anomaly appears, this time in relation to the goods workings:(see below)

As no goods or mixed service is shown in the up direction it is likely that one of the passenger services ran as a mixed service, probably the 4.05 pm. ex-Marlborough.

By early 1880 an additional return trip was provided on Thursdays only - Marlborough Market Day, allied to which there is still no mention of any up goods working. The timings of certain of the other services were also altered slightly to correspond with changes in the timings of the main line services: (see over)

	P	P	P	P	P	P
Marlborough	8.25am	9.10am	12.40pm	4.05pm	5.45pm	8.35pm
Savernake	8.40am	9.25am	12.55pm	4.20pm	6.00pm	8.50pm
	P&G	**P**	**P&G**	**P**	**P**	**P**
Savernake	8.48am	9.40am	1.20pm	4.45pm	6.20pm	9.13pm
Marlborough	9.03am	9.55am	1.35pm	5.00pm	6.35pm	9.28pm

A charming view of the original Marlborough branch service, in the bay at Savernake station in 1919. The locomotive is believed to be a 517 class 0-4-2T, whilst both coaches would appear to be four wheeled composite vehicles. Although almost hidden from view the starting signal for the train to leave is in the 'off' position. Notice also the backing signal at the end of the platform which applied to movements reversing from the up platform. When lowered this allowed empty trains to propel rearwards but only under the control of the shunter or guard. The wooden arm was replaced by an elevated 'dummy' during the 1950s. On the right hand side of the cutting, hidden by the train, are the sites of the second known signal box and also the pump house. From inside the latter it was possible to descend, by ladder, to the canal tunnel. The base of the former signal box survived for a number of years and was used as an office. In the background the original transfer (canal) siding can also be seen. Official references to this siding raise a number of questions; it was for instance stated that 'traffic for the MSWJ station at Marlborough will be transferred in the GWR yard at Savernake whilst traffic for north of Marlborough will travel over the GWR branch and be transferred to the MSWJ at that station.' The implication is that with limited sidings at Savernake very little exchange of traffic must have occurred; at Marlborough it may be taken to mean the movement of vehicles between the two stations. Was there then some form of 'trip' working at one time between them?

	P	P	P	P	P	P	P
Marlborough	8.20am	9.10am	10.40am	12.30pm	4.05pm	5.45pm	8.35pm
Savernake	8.40am	9.25am	10.54am	12.45pm	4.20pm	6.00pm	8.50pm
	P&G	P	P	P&G	P	P	P
Savernake	8.48am	9.40am	12.15pm	1.20pm	4.45pm	6.20pm	9.13pm
Marlborough	9.03am	9.55am	12.30pm	1.35pm	5.00pm	6.35pm	9.28pm

Narrow Gauge. **SAVERNAKE to MARLBOROUGH.** Single Line.

WEEK DAYS.

Down Trains.

Distances.	STATIONS.	1	2	3	4	5	B 6	7	8	C 9	10	11	12	13	14	15	16	17	18
		G. W. Goods.	M. & S. W. Mixed.	G. W. Passenger.	G. W. Passenger.	G. W. Passenger.			M. & H. W. Passenger.	M. & S. W. Passenger.	G. W. Goods.	G. W. Passenger.	G. W. Passenger.	M. & S. W. Passenger.	G. W. Passenger.	M. & S. W. Passenger.	M. & S. W. Passenger.	G. W. Passenger.	

		AM.	AM.	AM.	AM.	AM.			AM.	AM.	AM.	P.M.	P.M.	P.M.	P.M.	P.M.	P.M.	P.M.	
	Savernake ....dep.	6 45	7 8	8 40	9 35	10X 5	11 5		12	3 12	1 0	1 25		4 35	5 X 0	6 17	7 44	9 17	....
5¼	Marlborough Sth. Junc.	7 4	7X22	8 54	9X49	10 17	11 24		1214	12 26	1 20	1 39		4X49	5 18	6X31	7 56	9 29	....
5¾	Marlborough ....arr.	7 5		8 55	9 50		11 25			12 27		1 40		4 50		6 32		9 30	....

MARLBOROUGH to SAVERNAKE.

Narrow Gauge. Single Line.

WEEK DAYS.

Up Trains.

Distances.	STATIONS.	1	2	3	4	5	6	C 7	B 8	9	10	11	12	13	14	15	16	17	18
		G. W. Goods.	M. & S. W. Passenger.	G. W. Passenger.	G. W. Passenger.	M. & S. W. Passenger.			G. W. Passenger.	G. W. Passenger.	G. W. Goods.	G. W. Passenger.	M. & S. W. Passenger.	M. & H. W. Passenger.	G. W. Passenger.	M. & S. W. Passenger.	G. W. Mixed.	G. W. Passenger.	

		AM.	AM.	AM.	AM.	AM.			AM.	AM.		AM.	P.M.	P.M.	P.M.	P.M.	P.M.	P.M.	P.M.
	Marlborough ....dep.	6 15		8 15	9 10				10 30	10 25		12 35	12 36	2 24	4	5 50			8 45
	Marlborough Sth. Junc.	6 16	7X22	8 16	9 11	9X52			10 32	10 26		12 36	12 36	2 24	4 6	4X31	5 51	6X34	8 23	8 46
5¼	Savernake ....arr.	6 35	7 36	8 30	9 25	10X 4			10 45	10 45		12X50	2 38	4 20	5 X 2	6 5	6 54	8 35	8 58

B Not on Thursday. All Trains from Marlborough must approach Savernake cautiously. C Thursdays only.

Savernake to Marlborough.	SUNDAYS—Down Trains.				Marlborough to Savernake.	SUNDAYS—Up Trains.			
STATIONS.	1	2	3	4	STATIONS.	1	2	3	4
	M. & S. W Passngr.			M. & S. W Passngr.		M. & S. W. Passngr.			M. & S. W Passngr.
	AM.			PM.		AM.			PM.
Savernake ......dep.	11 1	....	....	7 50	Marlborough ....dep.	....	....	....	5 30
Marlborough Sth. Jun.	11 15	....	....	8 10	Marlborough Sth. Jun	8 23	....	....	5 30
Marlborough ......arr.					Savernake ....arr.	8 35	....	....	5 42

The Single Line between Savernake and Marlborough is worked by Train Staff, assisted by Disc Block Telegraph.

The following are the Staffs and Tickets:—	From	To	Shape.	Colour of Staff and Ticket.
	Savernake.	Marlborough Sth. Junction.	Triangular.	Yellow.
	Marlborough Sth. Junction.	Marlborough Station.	Round.	White.

CROSSING ARRANGEMENTS.

The 7.8 a.m. Mixed Train from Savernake crosses 7.22 a.m. Passenger Train from Marlborough South Junction at Marlborough South Junction.

The 9.35 a.m. Passenger Train from Savernake crosses the 9.52 a.m. Passenger Train from Marlborough South Junction at Marlborough South Junction.

The 10.5 a.m. Passenger Train from Savernake crosses 9.52 a.m. Passenger Train from Marlborough South Junction at Marlborough South Junction.

The 12.35 p.m. Passenger from Marlborough crosses 1.0 p.m. S. M. & A. Goods from Savernake at Savernake.

The 4.35 p.m. Passenger Train from Savernake crosses 4.51 p.m. S. M. & A. Pasr. from South Junction at South Junction.

The 4.51 p.m. Passenger from South Junction crosses 5.6 p.m. Passenger from Savernake at Savernake.

The 6.17 p.m. Passenger Train from Savernake crosses 6.34 p.m. Goods Train from Marlborough South Junction at South Junction.

An interesting variation in the normal branch services commenced with the advent of SMA traffic in 1883 which can be seen from the accompanying timetable of January 1885. At this time the passenger workings were fairly uniformly spread throughout the day with the exception of a three hour gap in the afternoon, when there was no down working.

Five years later in June 1890 the service had increased to a maximum of seventeen trains each way daily with twelve of these originating on the SMA. A natural break in the branch service occurred at Marlborough after the arrival of the 1.40 pm from Savernake and with the next GWR departure not due until 3.27 it is possible that this time was utilised either for engine purposes or as a shift change between engine crews. Still there was no Sunday service from the GWR terminus.

By 1895 branch trains had reached their peak, a maximum of 21 (8) down and 23 (9) up services - the figures in brackets refer to SMA services. From the timetable it can be seen for the first time that this also included an up GWR empty stock working; bearing in mind the rural nature of the line it is likely that passengers may well have been conveyed when necessary. The branch goods service does of course pose a question; siding accommodation at Savernake was limited - where might vehicles be stored at that station pending further movement?

In many respects the SMA station and route at Marlborough was able to offer better facilities for long distance traffic to and from the town as it was not hampered by the necessary detour though Newbury or Reading. Certainly there was no love lost between the GWR and SMA systems over such traffic. This transmitted itself to their respective staff members who would ignore the others' existence. Such animosity may appear slightly strange today, but it must be recalled that this was a time when men were far more loyal to their employers than is the practice today; it transcended the normal working day to cover a man's whole lifestyle. As an example it may be appropriate to quote an example from T.B. Sands, the story of a young man whose father was a ganger on the GWR near Savernake. The son announced he had been able to secure a position on the SMA, his father replying that as his son was going to work for the opposition he had better start by finding somewhere new to live. Today also we may smile perhaps at the antics of the great GWR General Manager, Sir Felix Pole; he lived in Ramsbury near Marlborough in 1891 and going to Swindon for interview with the GWR elected to travel via Hungerford Newbury and Didcot rather than more directly over SMA metals.

By July 1900 the Marlborough railway had of course reverted to true branch line status although still with a high level of service. Indeed in the down direction there were now nine passenger, two mixed and a maximum of three goods trains. The first two categories were reduced by one on weekdays (except Thursdays) whilst the normal single goods service if needed would also entail a light engine and van movement in the opposite direction. Traffic in the up direcion consisted of ten passenger trains - two of which ran Thursdays only, one goods

This additional train does prompt some thought, for the arrival at 12.30 pm at Marlborough corresponds exactly with the scheduled departure time for the next service! Again no Sunday trains are shown. During the various layovers at either end of the line, the branch engine would be occupied in shunting or pumping water, 'as required.'

Over the 1880 Easter Holiday the Great Western advertised the running of a number of through excursion trains to and from London, which applied to the period 25th March to 2nd April. In connection with this a special train ran from Devizes to London and return on Easter Monday, 29th March, which included a service leaving Marlborough at 6.10 am. This then connected with the special which arrived at Savernake at 6.37 am and following a number of other stops eventually arrived at Paddington at 9.30 am. The return working departed from London at 6.50 pm arriving Savernake 9.43 pm and Marlborough at 10.05.

SAVERNAKE TO MARLBOROUGH.

SINGLE LINE

Single Line worked by Electric Train Staff.

	DOWN TRAINS.		WEEK DAYS.																							SUNDAYS	
Distances.		1	2	3	4	5	6	7	8	9	10	11	12	13	14	15	16	17	18	19	20	21	22	23	24	1	2
	STATIONS.	A M.& S.W. Mxd.	D G.W. Goods	A G.W. Pass.	A G.W. Pass.	A M.& S.W. Pass.	A G.W. Mixed	A G.W. Mixed	D M.& S.W. Goods	A G.W. Pass.	A M.& S.W. Pass.	A G.W. Pass.	A G.W. Mixed	A G.W. Pass.	A M.& S.W. Pass.	A G.W. Pass.	A G.W. Pass.	A G.W. Pass.	A M.& S.W. Pass.	A G.W. Pass.	A G.W. Pass.	A G.W. Pass.	A G.W. Pass.			D M.& S.W. Goods	A M.& S.W. Pass.
							L	K			L				L													
M|C		A.M.	A.M.	A.M.	A.M.	A.M.	A.M.	A.M.	A.M.	A.M.	A.M.	P.M.	P.M.	P.M.	P.M.	P.M.	P.M.	P.M.	P.M.	P.M.	P.M.	P.M.	P.M.			P.M.	P.M.
—	Savernake dep.	6 X 5	6X50	8 30	9 35	9 J47	10 50	11 10	11X27	11 38	12 7	12 47	1 50	3 7	3J35	4X15	5	5 26	6 39	7X25	7 37	8 32	9 25	..		11 10	12 1	7 58
24	M'rlbro' S.J. „	6X20	7 X 9	8 42	9 47	9X57	11 4	11 24	11X40	11X47	12X19	12 59	2 X 4	3 15	—	4 27	5 14	5X38	6 51	7 37	7X49	8 44	9 37	...		11 22	12 15	8 10
5 49	Marlboro' arr		7 10	8 43	9 48		11 5	11 25		11 48		1 0	2 5	3 20	3X45	4 28	5 15		6 52	7 38		8 45	9 38	..			12 15	
									N																			

	UP TRAINS.		WEEK DAYS.																							SUNDAYS	
Distances.		1	2	3	4	5	6	7	8	9	10	11	12	13	14	15	16	17	18	19	20	21	22	23	24	1	2
	STATIONS.	D M.& S.W. Goods	D G.W. Goods	A M.& S.W. Pass. Sats. only.	A M.& S.W. Pass.	A G.W. Pass.	A G.W. Pass.	A M.& S.W. Mxd.	A G.W. Mixed	A G.W. Pass.	A G.W. Pass.	A G.W. Pass.	A M.& S.W. Pass.	A G.W. Pass.	A G.W. Pass.	A M.& S.W. Pass.	A G.W. Pass.	A G.W. Pass.	D M.& S.W. Goods	A G.W. Mixed	A G.W. Pass.	A M.& S.W. Mixed	A G.W. Em'pty Pass.	A G.W. Pass.		A M.& S.W. Pass.	A M.& S.W. Pass.
							L						L															
M|C		A.M.	A.M.	A.M.	A.M.	A.M.	A.M.	A.M.	A.M.	A.M.	A.M.	P.M.	P.M.	P.M.	P.M.	P.M.	P.M.	P.M.	P.M.	P.M.	P.M.	P.M.	P.M.	P.M.		A.M.	P.M.
—	Marlboro' dep.		5 50	—	—	8 0	9 5	—	10 20	11 15	—	12 20	1 20	....	2 35	3 50	—	4 35	—	6 57	0	—	8 10	8 55	....		
25	M'rlbro' S.J. „	5 15	5 51	6X25	7X11	8 1	9 6	9X57	10 21	11 16	11X47	12X21	1 21	2 X 4	2 36	3X51	4 3	4 36	5X38	6 6	7 1	7X57	8 11	8 56	...	8 23	5 30
5 49	Savernake arr.	5 30	6X 5	6X35	7 22	8 13	9 18	10 9	10 33	11X27	11J57	12 33	1 33	2 16	2 48	4 3	J4X14	4 48	5 58	6 20	7X13	8 10	8 23	9 8	....	8 35	5 42

J Calls at Savernake when required.   K Thursdays excepted.   L Thursdays only.

N On Thursdays this Train must leave Savernake at 1.0 p.m. and arrive at Marlborough South Junction at 1.15 p.m.   Maximum load—10 Mineral 15 Mixed.

All Trains from Marlborough must approach Savernake cautiously.

	am	am	am	am	pm	pm	pm	pm	pm	pm	pm
Marlboro	7.52	9.03	10.25	11.15	12.37	1.30	2.40	4.17	5.57	6.55	7.47
Savernake	8.05	9.16	10.38	11.27	12.50	1.43	2.53	4.30	6.12	7.07	7.50
Savernake	8.22	9.35	10.52	11.37	1.08*	2.00	3.05	5.02*	6.35	7.18	8.12
Marlboro	8.35	9.48	11.05	11.50	1.21*	2.15	3.18	5.15*	6.47	7.30	8.25

*Thursdays only.

The 11.37am, 2.00pm and 5.57pm services were advertised as mixed.

train - two on Thursdays and one mixed train.

The 1902 timetable suggests an amount of economy had been effected although not to any particularly striking degree:

Some time between 1902 and 1905 a single Sunday service was instigated for the movement of milk, scheduled to be operated by an engine and van leaving Savernake at 7.20 pm and arriving at Marlborough thirteen minutes later. Just twelve minutes were allowed at the terminus for running round and loading with departure scheduled for 7.45 pm and arrival at Savernake at 7.59 pm. With the engine coming from elsewhere it must be asked - how was a runround effected at the terminus? As we have seen the normal practice was to stable the branch coaches in the platform.*

A statistical count of the number of trains using the line during the month of July 1906 makes for interesting reading:

Between	and	pass	gds
Bedwyn	**Grafton Curve Jct.**	969	321
Grafton Curve Jct	**MSWJ**	2	2
Grafton Curve Jct	**Wolfhall Jct.**	967	967
Wolfhall Jct.	**Savernake Station**	967	321
Savernake Station	**Marlboro Bch. Jct.**	1606	364
Marlboro Bch. Jct.	**Burbage**	952	311
Burbage	**Pewsey**	952	311

The actual number of trains during this period can thus be assessed, referring to 654 passenger and 53 goods services. (One may perhaps wonder how this information was compiled - from the signal box train registers or by men sat along the line at intervals!)

The Sunday milk service ceased in May 1910 but apart from four additional trains shown as 'running if required' the timetable was relatively unaltered.* These appeared ('as required') in the timetable as 'Q' paths. Bradshaw provides an

The locomotive for the Sunday working came off the 5.35 pm Trowbridge to Paddington milk service which previously arrived at Savernake at 7.09 pm and departed at 8.09 pm. It collected milk from all stations from Trowbridge to Newbury running via Holt and Devizes and then ran to Paddington, calling only at Reading.

It is not clear how the Sunday milk traffic was handled during the periods when no Sunday service was operated. Possibly an arrangement was arrived at whereby a carrier would deliver the milk direct to Savernake.

interesting indication to passengers, declaring that additional services between Marlborough and Savernake were available by the M&SWJ - probably the only publication where the existence of the rival's services were publicly acknowledged!

In connection with the 'economic system of maintenance' introduced on the branch in August 1910 a further, albeit less detailed census of traffic was taken, revealing that on weekdays between 6.00 am and 5.30 pm there were 16 regular trains and two occasional services. Over the 24 hour period the figures were 22 and 4 respectively.

In response to a serious Miner's Strike an emergency timetable was introduced on the London Division of the GWR from 18th August 1911, in which a number of trains were curtailed. As far as the Marlborough branch was concerned this involved the cancellation of the late evening passenger service to Savernake and return. It has not been possible to discover how long this remained the case.

Presumably in some response to wartime loadings a late night passenger service was introduced for the first time in July 1915, running on Wednesdays and Saturdays only. It is believed to have left Savernake at 9.05 pm arriving at Marlborough at 9.26. The return working departed the terminus at 10.02 pm arriving on the main line at 10.38. The implication is that an engine off a main line train was used, whilst the apparently lengthy journey time for just over five miles is open to question. A note in the timetable stated .. 'this service will not run after 29.9.1915'.

At the same period the Sunday milk service was restored; this time a Marlborough engine was used with the train advertised as 'passenger and milk', leaving Marlborough at 6.33 pm to arrive at Savernake 6.45 pm. The return working departed Savernake at 8.03 pm to reach the terminus at 8.15 pm. The milk was then taken forward by an up train which left the junction station at 8.10 pm. It is not known how long the Sunday service was retained or if the late night working was resurrected the following year.

By 1916 the passenger service provided nine regular trains each way, all of these terminating at Savernake. Other than certain of the slip coach workings referred to later in this chapter it is not thought there were ever any regular through passenger trains in either direction; exceptions were of course the special services run at the beginning and end of term at Marlborough College.

SAVERNAKE TO MARLBOROUGH.

The goods service was run during the afternoon lull in activity with the timetable arranged for the operation of the service with just one engine. Restrictions were placed on the number of vehicles that could be taken per trip and the average freight load for the period was made up of seven vehicles; the maximum number permitted, regardless of type, was 25 empties. This figure decreased according to the weight of the train, 24 mixed freight vehicles, 22 goods vehicles or 13 loaded coal wagons. In all cases the weight of the goods van was included.

With trains worked only by tank engines, restricted to a 'yellow' axle loading, there were relatively few different engine types to be seen on the branch. The goods service was later retimed, so that by 1920 it operated during the late evening, after the last passenger working. The first train of the morning in either direction also ran as a mixed service and it is believed these arrangements persisted more or less until closure to passengers in 1933.

1916 Weekdays only

	am	am	am	pm	pm	pm	pm	pm	pm
Marlborough	7.40	9.05	10.25	12.12	12.57	1.47	4.25	5.45	7.30
Savernake	7.53	9.18	10.38	12.25	1.09	2.00	4.38	5.58	7.42
Savernake	8.12	9.32	11.20	12.40	1.18	2.18	5.15	6.43	8.05
Marlborough	8.24	9.45	11.33	12.52	1.30	2.30	5.57	6.55	8.18

GWR Savernake - Marlborough

	am	am	am	pm	pm	pm	pm	pm	pm
Savernake	8.30	9.45	11.15	1.10	2.40	5.15	6.07	7.05	8.30
Marlborough	8.45	10.00	11.27	1.22	2.52	5.30	6.19	7.20	8.42
Marlborough	7.25	9.05	10.50	12.30	2.10	4.10	5.45	6.32	7.55
Savernake	7.37	9.17	11.02	12.42	2.22	4.25	5.47	6.47	8.07

The similarity between services is obvious, illustrated in particular by the timings of the last Savernake - Marlborough trains, booked to leave within one minute of each other.

GWR branch timetables for the mid-1920s show little change from the 1922 service with the exception of an additional mid-afternoon train, where there had previously been a lengthy gap.

By the summer of 1930 the first signs of a contraction in the service had appeared with the removal of the evening (8.05 pm) train Marlborough to Savernake and return. Despite this the goods service retained its late evening schedule.

In the public timetable for 1932 - the last full year of the branch service - the duplication between GWR and former M&SWJ routes appears at last to have partly resolved, whilst the timings of the road motor services are also given. It also shows a gap of over five hours between rail services from Savernake to Marlborough High Level after 11.17 am. In the working book however two 'Q' paths are indicated:

Marlborough 12.32 pm 2.05 pm
Savernake 12.44 pm 2.17 pm

Savernake 1.05 pm 2.30 pm
Marlborough 1.17 pm 2.42 pm

It is not certain what conditions had to apply before these services would operate or how much notice would be given. An additional factor hardly likely to improve the standing of the railway with the local community was that the 10.55 am from Marlborough and corresponding return working from Savernake at 11.17 am did not run between 17th September and 3rd June! At worst then this could result in a seven hour daytime gap between trains on the original branch; hardly likely to improve receipts.

The main line through Savernake was itself in the earliest days little more than an elongated branch line; trains on the Marlborough line were nevertheless timed to connect with the main line services whenever possible and accordingly reflected the service provided on the Berks and Hants route. In June 1865 for example there were just four trains each way through Savernake on weekdays with two on Sundays. Most of these were Paddington to Weymouth services (running via Devizes, Holt and Westbury) though there was also the occasional Paddington to Bristol train - a devious route between the two places rewarding the unsuspecting traveller with the prospect of a journeytime not far short of 4½ hours!

With the general upgrading of the main line and subsequent opening of the Stert & Westbury and Somerton cut-offs, main line traffic increased, even though a number of these trains were not scheduled to call at Savernake.

In 1902 there were some ten passenger trains passing Savernake in each direction and by 1910 these included six up line stopping services and seven on the down line. Two stopping passenger trains ran each way on Sundays. The figure for weekday trains passing through the station had trebled by 1932, whilst during the Bank Holiday and summer peak periods trains ran almost in a nose to tail succession.

Some of the most intriguing workings at Savernake relate to the slip coach services first introduced in July 1902 with a vehicle off the 5.00 pm Paddington - Weymouth express. By July 1906 six trains were booked to slip at Savernake, the first three of these down Weymouth trains leaving Paddington at 9.55 am, 12.35 pm and 5.00 pm. A coach was also slipped from the 3.00 pm Paddington - Bristol via Devizes service. The summer only 11.10 am Paddington - Penzance also slipped, at 12.25 pm, with Savernake the only intermediate station served by this train on its non-stop run to Exeter. From 14th July 1906 there was a slip coach working in the up direction, off the 12.17 pm ex-Ilfracombe service, passing Savernake at 4.23 pm.

Apart from the 5.00 pm from Paddington due at Savernake at 6.35, all the slip coaches ran directly into the platform and were then taken forward by local train. The 5.00 pm Weymouth train was brought to a stand by the East Signal Box where the slip coach was detached, to be brought into the station on a down stopping service which had arrived at Savernake earlier and was waiting in the down relief siding. In the other cases the local train would probably be standing 'wrong-road' on the down main line.

A number of alterations were made to the timing and number of slips at Savernake over the years but by November 1911 they had declined to just two. A third was reinstated shortly afterwards.

A surviving record for the period, 4th May 1914 to 11th July 1914, reveals the three slip services to have survived:

GWR Working of Slip Coaches;
Working No. 11 - commences 30th May.

9.35 am Paddington to Savernake (slip)
11.20 am Savernake to Marlborough
12.08 pm Marlborough to Savernake
1.30 pm Savernake to Hungerford
2.18 pm Hungerford to Paddington

Working No 31 - single ended vehicle to be used

6.30 am Trowbridge to Paddington
5.00 pm Paddington to Savernake (slip)
6.45 pm Savernake to Trowbridge

SLIPPING OF COACHES.

Slipping Point for Slips running to Platform. Down Refuge Siding Stop Blocks.

„   „   „   stopping at East Box Home Signal. Down Distant Signal for East Box.

There is a Catch Point in the Down Main Line, about 650 yards outside the Down Home Signal for East Box, and about 25 yards inside the Down Distant Signal, for East Box.

Coaches when slipped off a Down Train at Savernake to go forward by a local Train shunted in Refuge Siding, must **not** be run direct to the Down Platform, but must be stopped at the Down Home Signal for the East Signal Box.

The local Train booked to shunt at Savernake for the through Train to pass must, after its work has been completed at the Platform, be shunted back into the Down Refuge Siding, and the Guard must go back with it, where it must be stopped opposite the fencing put up between the Siding and Canal Bank.

When the slip off Through Train has come to a stand, the local Train will draw out of the Refuge Siding and back on to the slip on the Down Main Line. The Train and the slip will then draw up to the Platform.

The Down Refuge Siding must in such cases be kept sufficiently clear for the local Train to be shunted into when necessary.

Working No 62

12.25 pm Paddington to Savernake (slip)
2.06 pm Savernake to Marlborough
3.20 pm Marlborough to Savernake
3.38 pm Savernake to Reading
7.14 am Reading to Paddington

In all cases the slip portion comprised only a single vehicle.

The last of the slip coach workings to survive at Savernake came off the 12.25 pm Weymouth service; it ceased as a result of the war on 31st December 1916, along with the rest of the slip services throughout the GWR. Whilst a number were later resumed elsewhere none were reinstated at Savernake.

At its peak passengers for Marlborough could benefit from the slip coach service and it is likely they were first introduced as a result of certain influential persons in the area. Of course in the reverse direction no such fast service was provided and London bound passengers from Marlborough would be faced with a change of train first at Savernake and then (usually) again at either Newbury or Reading.

An odd working reported in 1914 concerned a steam railmotor on a daily schedule from Frome to Hungerford. This vehicle was shedded at Frome and waited at Savernake in the up direction from 1.01 pm to 1.30 pm daily - connecting with the lunchtime arrival from Marlborough. The railmotor service on this route lasted for a number of years, at least until 1921 though there is no evidence to suggest that steam railmotors were ever used on the Marlborough branch itself.

Perhaps surprisingly and despite such direct competition for the same traffic, receipts for the branch appeared to hold up well. The GWR traffic statistics for 1903 and 1913 are certainly at a respectable level. After this the figures are complicated by the effects of inflation and corrected for this show a gradual decline, even allowing for additional war time traffic. (regretfully figures for the period 1904 - 1912 are not available.)

A number of staff posed for the camera at the main entrance to the station. Although undated, the photograph probably derives from the early years of the present century, and what may well be a slip-coach from Paddington stands at the platform. A gas-tank wagon ('cordon') was stabled at Marlborough, used as a reservoir to re-fill the gas cylinders of the branch coaches. Special pathing arrangements were provided in the working timetable for the 'cordon' to be returned to Swindon when empty and a replenished wagon provided.

APPENDIX ONE

MARLBOROUGH LOCOMOTIVE ALLOCATIONS

No details available prior to 1873.

8th December 1873:-
Tank engines *HORACE* - ' Bogie class ' and *THISTLE* - ' Metro class '.

From 1902 and until the shed closed in 1933, details of the locomotives allocated to Marlborough are given in a series of contemporary record books of GWR locomotive stock and available for inspection at the Public Record Office under the reference RAIL 254/61 et.seq. These books provide a numerical list of GWR locomotives giving their allocation during a particular four week period although it naturally follows that changes took place continually and not just at the start and end of a four week cycle. Each location is identified by a standard abbreviation, with the reference *MARLBO* used to avoid confusion with Marlow.
It follows then that changes of allocation to suit operational needs occured as required and the allocation lists must then be seen as identifying only a moment in time. Engines would sometimes spend a year or more at a particular depot whilst others may only have stood in for a day or even less. This then helps to explain the lack of obvious continuity of dates.
At times when no allocation is given it may be stated this was when relief motive power was provided.
Prior to 1923, relief engines were supplied from Trowbridge but upon closure of that shed it is believed replacements were then provided by the depots at either Westbury or Swindon.
It would also appear that two engines were usually based at Marlborough shed. The types used were those typically found on minor branch lines and often included locomotives unsuitable for more exacting duties and were *past their prime*. An example of this may be No. 573 of 1915 and which on the 20th February was sent from Marlborough to Swindon and condemned after serving just a year on the branch.

Note - For clarity the following list is given in numerical sequence only. Allocation dates, when known, are given alongside.

Year	No.	Class		Type	Dates
1902	519	**517**	class	0-4-2T	up to 25/1
	551	'	'	'	from 8/3
1903	519	'	'	'	from 19/9
	551	'	'	'	from 19/9
1904	522	'	'	'	up to 5/3
	551	'	'	'	up to 5/3
1905	522	'	'	'	all year
1906	522	'	'	'	up to 6/1
	546	'	'	'	from 28/4 to 28/6
	1423	'	'	'	from 30/6
1907	1423	'	'	'	all year
1908	534	'	'	'	from 12/5
	1423	'	'	'	to 23/5 & from 20/6
1909	218	'	'	'	from 27/5
	534	'	'	'	up to 19/6
	1423	'	'	'	up to 19/6
1910	218	'	'	'	all year
	534	'	'	'	up to 26/2
	1470	'	'	'	from 26/2
1911	218	'	'	'	all year
	629	**Metro**	class	2-4-0T	from 18/2 to 10/3
	1476	**517**	class	0-4-2T	all year
1912	218	'	'	'	up to 27/1
	829	'	'	'	by 27/1
	1476	'	'	'	to 20/2 & from 15/7 to 5/10
1913	829	'	'	'	all year
	839	'	'	'	all year
1914	573	'	'	'	from 21/2
	829	'	'	'	up to 24/1
	839	'	'	'	all year
	1150	**1076**	class	0-6-0T	from 24/1 to 21/3
1915	519	**517**	class	0-4-2T	from 20/2 to 27/11
	551	'	'	'	from 27/11
	573	'	'	'	up to 20/2
	835	'	'	'	from 2/10 to 27/11
	839	'	'	'	up to 2/10
	1484	'	'	'	from 5/11
1916	551	'	'	'	all year
	1484	'	'	'	all year
1917	551	'	'	'	all year
	1484	'	'	'	all year
1918	551	'	'	'	up to 16/2
	1479	'	'	'	from 26/10
	1484	'	'	'	up to 26/10
1919	1479	'	'	'	up to 25/10
1920	Records missing.				
1921	739	**1076**	class	0-6-0T	from 19/6 to 17/7 & 11/9 to 9/10
	835	**517**	class	0-4-2T	from 27/3 to 22/5
	986	**Metro**	class	2-4-0T	from 27/2 to 27/3 & 22/5 to 19/6
	1446	'	'	'	from 12/1 to 27/3
	1565	**1076**	class	0-6-0T	from 24/4 to 22/5 also 17/7 to 14/8 & from 9/10
	1624	'	'	'	from 16/8 to 11/9

Year	No.	Class		Type	Dates
1922	1565	'	'	'	all year
1923	739	'	'	'	from 25/3 to 22/4 & 20/5 to 17/6
	1565	'	'	'	up to 25/3
	1566	'	'	'	from 21/2
	1603	'	'	'	from 22/4 to 20/5 & 9/9 to 2/12
	1650	'	'	'	from 17/6 to 9/9
1924	986	**Metro**	class	2-4-0T	from 15/6 to 27/1
	1565	**1076**	class	0-6-0T	from 18/5 to 15/6, 13/7 to 10/8, 7/9 to 5/10, 2/11 to 30/11 & from 28/12
	1566	'	'	'	up to 27/1
	1603	'	'	'	from 27/1 to 23/3 & 20/4 to 18/5
	1827	**1813**	class	0-6-0T	from 30/11 to 28/12
1925	1228	**1076**	class	0-6-0T	from 9/8 to 1/11
	1290	'	'	'	from 17/5 to 12/7
	1291	'	'	'	from 27/12
	1565	'	'	'	up to 22/2
	1566	'	'	'	from 22/2 to 19/4 & 1/11 to 27/12
	1652	'	'	'	from 12/7 to 9/8
	1827	**1813**	class	0-6-0T	from 19/4 to 17/5
1926	613	**Metro**	class	2-4-0T	from 3/10 to 31/10
	986	'	'	'	from 24/1 to 22/2, 18/4 to 16/5 & 11/7 to 5/9
	1291	**1076**	class	0-6-0T	up to 24/1 & 16/5 to 13/6
	1413	**Metro**	class	2-4-0T	from 5/9 to 13/10 & from 28/11
	1491	'	'	'	from 31/10 to 28/11
1927	638	**633**	class	0-6-0T	from 27/11 to 25/12
	986	**Metro**	class	2-4-0T	from 20/2 to 15/5 & from 25/12
	1413	'	'	'	up to 20/2, from 15/5 to 12/6 & 4/9 to 2/10
	1453	'	'	'	from 7/8 to 4/9
	1457	'	'	'	from 12/6 to 10/7 & 30/10 to 27/11
	1603	**1076**	class	0-6-0T	from 10/7 to 7/8
1928	460	**Metro**	class	2-4-0T	from 28/10 to 23/11
	638	**633**	class	0-6-0T	from 19/2 to 18/3, 15/4 to 10/6 & 30/9 to 28/10
	735	**1076**	class	0-6-0T	from 10/6 to 5/8
	751	'	'	'	from 5/8 to 2/9
	986	**Metro**	class	2-4-0T	up to 19/2
	1134	**1076**	class	0-6-0T	from 2/9 to 30/9 & 25/11 to 23/12
	1457	**Metro**	class	2-4-0T	from 18/3 to 15/4
1929	460	'	'	'	from 9/6 to 7/7 & 4/8 to 29/9
	638	**633**	class	0-6-0T	from 20/1 to 17/2 & 12/5 to 9/6
	751	**1076**	class	0-6-0T	up to 20/1
	1499	**Metro**	class	2-4-0T	from 17/2 to 12/5, 7/7 to 4/8, 29/9 to 27/10 & from 24/11
1930	613	'	'	'	from 2/8 to 27/9 & 22/11 to 20/12
	1135	**1076**	class	0-6-0T	from 18/1 to 15/2 & 7/6 to 5/7
	1494	**Metro**	class	2-4-0T	from 15/2 to 12/4 & 25/10 to 22/11
	1499	'	'	'	up to 18/1
	1738	**1854**	class	0-6-0T	from 20/12
	2047	**2021**	class	0-6-0T	from 12/4 to 7/6, 5/7 to 2/8 & 27/9 to 25/10
1931	1135	**1076**	class	0-6-0T	from 14/2 to 14/3
	1494	**Metro**	class	2-4-0T	from 17/1 to 14/2
	1738	**1854**	class	0-6-0T	up to 17/1, 11/4 to 9/5 & 6/6 to 1/8
	1758	'	'	'	from 9/5 to 4/7, 1/8 to 26/9 & 24/10 to 21/11
	1761	'	'	'	from 26/9 to 24/10 & from 21/11
	2744	**2721**	class	0-6-0T	from 14/3 to 11/4
1932	1731	**1854**	class	0-6-0T	from 22/10
	1738	'	'	'	from 12/3 to 9/4, 4/6 to 30/7 & 24/9 to 22/10
	1758	'	'	'	from 13/2 to 12/3
	1761	'	'	'	up to 13/2, 9/4 to 4/6 & 30/7 to 27/8
	2744	**2721**	class	0-6-0T	from 27/8 to 24/9
1933	Records missing.				

APPENDIX TWO

TRAFFIC HANDLED PRIOR TO 1900

Figures compiled from official Marlborough Railway Records. Gaps are as they appear in the original register. (Public Record Office references: *RAIL 470/9, 470/10 and 470/11.*)

TICKETS ISSUED.

Period ending.	Single			Return			Excursion		Soldiers	Car'ges	Horses	Dogs
	1st.	2nd.	3rd.	1st.	2nd.		1st.	2nd.				
30- 4-1864	107	442	375	64	360		26	241	2		14	3
31-12-1864	174	968	980	50	422		12	40	9	2	13	9
30- 6-1865	185	1262	1369	110	494		50	994	12	2	23	3
31-12-1865	159	1102	1105	84	544		3	45	10	3	9	4
30- 6-1866	224	1090	990	154	536						9	3
31-12-1866	180	976	1137	110	492					1	4	1
30- 6-1867	191	1114	1231	158	438		64	874		2	25	5
31-12-1867	190	1030	987	140	446		2	25			2	7
30- 6-1868	217	1243	1155	140	570		4	112			17	6
31-12-1868	190	1127	948	44	305		3	17			21	7
30- 6-1869	195	1472	1127	66	315							
31-12-1869	186	1063	909	67	302			16		1	20	5
30- 6-1870	141	858	1156	55	320					1	42	3
31-12-1870	232	1244	1146	53	340		4	30		1	8	9
30- 6-1871	321	1469	1838	63	309		5	54			51	3
31-12-1871	189	1269	1182	44	390		2	22		1	3	9
30- 6-1872	209	690	2430	51	161		5	47			58	1
31-12-1872	213	699	2899	45	107		3	19			7	10
30- 6-1873	174	410	3291	96	191			34		6	54	14
31-12-1873	209	828	3290	53	146					3	14	15
30- 6-1874	122	411	2861	54	173		4	62		4	33	13
31-12-1874	165	752	2068*	66	205		66	205		1	6	10
30- 6-1875	250	1923	675	123	260			24		2	62	10
31-12-1875	106	623	1958	76	295							
30- 6-1876	123	259	2450	95	381			20			66	15

* Illegible entry in register

Period ending	Single			Return			Excursion		Carriages	Horses	Dogs
	1st.	2nd.	3rd.	1st.	2nd.	3rd.	1st.	2nd.			
31-12-1876	66	670	2210	64	299	35			2	9	16
30- 6-1877	102	257	2011	65	326	19		29		49	14
31-12-1877	443	2597	15092	401	1929	152		230		8	17
30- 6-1878	94	199	2602	107	366	20		28	2	69	7
31-12-1878	35	635	2020	51	331	22		29		14	6
30- 6-1879	57	223	2126	90	356	40		17		49	16
31-12-1879	597	2525	393	392	2018	303	3	326		31	8
30- 6-1880	71	243	2314	85	407	36		19	1	51	33
31-12-1880	37	406	2496	37	389	34		26		37	77

No reason is given for the exceptional figures appertaining to the period 31-12-1877.

Figures for period 1-1-1881 to 31-12-1890 and 1-7-1894 to 30-6-1897 not available.

Period ending.	Pass Tickets.	Warehouse Rent.	Carriages.	Horses.	Dogs.
30- 6-1891	5200	£00 - 16 - 1d	1	5	9
31-12-1891	5428	-	1	10	13
30- 6-1892	6038	-	6	57	19
31-12-1892	6103	£25 - 17 - 6d	1	1	35
30- 6-1893	7798	£19 - 5 - 0d	1	36	11
31-12-1893	5441	£22 - 17 - 0d	1	23	42
30- 6-1894	7004	£19 - 16 - 3d	2	28	16
31-12-1894	5877	£23 - 19 - 0d	1	7	19

In addition there is an unspecified amount, but thought to be in order of £2 - 18 - 0d per month obtained from Telegraph and Mail receipts.

Period ending	Tons.	No. of cattle.	Parcels In.
30- 6-1864	437	-	404
31-12-1864	496	11	1109
30- 6-1865	538	-	923
31-12-1865	678	-	1203
30- 6-1866	638	164	993
31-12-1866	806	-	1257
30- 6-1867	567	-	1119
31-12-1867	763	-	1333
30- 6-1868	676	93	986
31-12-1868	568	-	1327
30- 6-1869	824	32	1111
31-12-1869	887	8	1387
30- 6-1870	518	76	1257
31-12-1870	1194	-	1812

Period ending	Tons.	No. of cattle.	Parcels.
30- 6-1871	823	8	1126
31-12-1871	1292	9	1761
30- 6-1872	1251	30	1285
31-12-1872	850	-	1339
30- 6-1873	850	11	1364
31-12-1873	1011	80	1720
30- 6-1874	734	-	1358
31-12-1874	1130	-	1724
30- 6-1875	1136	33	1520
31-12-1875		No entries.	
30- 6-1876	891	53	1678
31-12-1876	961	-	1660
30- 6-1877	989	76	1631
31-12-1877	1120	200	1673
30- 6-1878	733	202	1656
31-12-1878	1076	27	1809
30- 6-1879	825	163	1437
31-12-1879	1625	55	2040
30- 6-1880	1282	130	1718
31-12-1880	1741	35	1916

Figures for period 1-1-881 to 31-12-1890 and 1-7-1894 to 30-6-1897 not available.

30- 6-1891	2579	38*	1092
31-12-1891	2610	81*	1498
30- 6-1892	2147	53*	1227
31-12-1892	4562	64*	1689
30- 6-1893	2262	113*	1370
31-12-1893	3593	76*1576	
30- 6-1894	3833	21*	1241
31-12-1897	4531	72*	1587

* From 30-6-1891 the figures relating to cattle movements are shown as referring to cattle wagons and not as previously entered i.e. actual number of beasts.

In addition, for the month of June 1865, £1 - 12 - 0d is shown accrued from Mail services.

Proportion of receipts due to Marlborough Rly Co.

30- 6-1891	£1054 - 6 - 8d
31-12-1891	£1186 - 11 - 8d
30- 6-1892	£1098 - 8 - 9d
31-12-1892	£1318 - 16 - 5d
30- 6-1893	£1139 - 17 - 4d
31-12-1893	£1290 - 19 - 3d
30- 6-1894	£1148 - 15 - 7d
31-12-1894	£1291 - 3 - 5d

The above figures are for the periods six months ending.

Figures for other periods not available.

APPENDIX 3

Traffic Statistics

Station.	Year.	Staff: Supervisory and Wages (all Grades).	Staff: Paybill Expenses.	Total Receipts.	Passenger Train Traffic: Tickets Issued.	Season Tickets.	Receipts: Passengers (including Season Tickets, etc.)	Receipts: Parcels.	Receipts: Miscellaneous.	Receipts: Total.
		No.	£	£	No.	No.	£	£	£	£
Savernake to Castle Cary.										
Savernake (Low Level)	1903	11	631	2,690	18 031	*	1 549	109	845	2,503
	1913	12	924	3,422	19,544	*	1,796	242	951	2,989
	1923	15	2,518	5 161	16,662	63	2,550	221	1,442	4 213
	1924	15	2,469	4,509	15,508	35	2 483	159	1,229	3,871
	1925	15	2 574	4,567	13,847	46	2,291	173	1 377	3,841
	1926	15	2,546	5,185	11,475	35	1,948	148	2,537	4,633
	1927	16	2,511	4,995	11,021	35	1,939	159	1,905	4,003
	1928	16	2,487	4,900	10,388	43	1,903	151	2,033	4,087
	1929	16	2,500	5,049	9,435	42	1,830	190	2,501	4,521
	1930	16	2,530	4,966	8,410	34	1,705	179	2,429	4,313
	1931	16	§2,351	5,554	8,436	25	1,854	148	2,864	4,866
	1932	15	§2,683	6,012	7,521	20	1,664	156	3,586	5,406
	1933	16	§2,405	5,159	8,016	18	1,514	195	2,885	4,594
Burbage Goods. (†)	1903			1,204						
	1913			1 048						
	1923	Included		3,722						
	1924	with		2,390						
	1925	Savernake		2 057						
	1926	Low Level.		2,204						
	1927			2,493						
	1928			2,295						
	1929			2,332						
	1930			1,885						
	1931			1,663						
	1932			1,259						
	1933			651						
		Taken over from Midland & S.W. Jct. Rly., October, 1923.								
Marlborough (‡)	1923	8	1,114	13,983	28,743	—	4,218	809	4,604	9,631
	1924	6	1,213	15,537	23,678	8	4,371	1,100	5,046	10,517
	1925	6	1,220	13,432	23,394	3	4,177	1,063	3,078	8,318
	1926	6	1,207	11,772	19,516	5	3,638	964	3,860	8,462
	1927	7	1,190	13,227	21,938	5	4,073	1,083	4,385	9,541
	1928	7	1,239	11,638	20,935	3	3,761	1,078	4,646	9,485
	1929	7	1,230	12,586	20,905	12	3,761	1,071	5,175	10,007
	1930	7	1,262	13,120	19,148	5	3,017	998	6,001	10,016
	1931	6	‖3,423	15,409	18,270	12	2,967	916	5,009	8,892
	1932	6	‖2,922	13,117	11,272	11	2,281	866	4,351	7,498
	1933	6	‖2,393	20,484	15,567	17	4,376	1,701	4,199	10,276
		Taken over from Midland & S.W. Jct., Rly., October, 1923.								
Savernake (High Level) (§)	1923	3	513	2,979	5,977	—	733	112	1,407	2,252
	1924	3	484	3,703	5,744	—	743	71	2,040	2,854
	1925	3	463	3,539	5,749	—	792	67	2,203	3,062
	1926	3	441	3,515	5,021	—	667	56	2,265	2,988
	1927	3	433	3,908	6,125	3	774	48	2,512	3,334
	1928	3	443	2,933	5,050	3	619	47	1,496	2,162
	1929	3	425	2,534	4,111	—	586	47	1,335	1,968
	1930	3	450	3,081	3,619	—	479	39	1,952	2,470
	1931	3	*	2,930	3,617	—	419	43	2,029	2,491
	1932	3	*	1,438	3,343	—	388	36	653	1,077
	1933	1	*	757	1,279	—	154	9	176	339
		Taken over from Midland & S.W. Jct. Rly., October, 1923.								
Grafton & Burbage.	1923	4	653	10,582	3,072	—	338	140	4,143	4,621
	1924	4	666	7,093	3,464	4	318	117	3,605	4,040
	1925	4	680	8,089	3,878	7	346	112	3,638	4,096
	1926	4	699	6,884	3,233	9	294	103	2,352	2 749
	1927	4	726	6,299	3,236	13	409	110	2,450	2,969
	1928	4	714	4,015	3,498	13	291	93	1,789	2,173
	1929	4	699	3,762	3,509	8	274	92	1,539	1,905
	1930	4	695	3,721	3,818	4	308	79	1,118	1,505
	1931	4	671	2,835	2,921	3	275	78	1,105	1,458
	1932	4	651	2,500	3,295	2	232	67	1,127	1,426
	1933	6	839	1,931	3,190	6	235	64	495	794

* Included with Savernake (Low Level). † Supervised by Marlborough from July, 1933. ‡ Controlled by Marlborough (High Level) to March, 1933. § Controlled by Savernake (Low Level). ‖ Includes Marlborough (High Level).

BRISTOL DIVISION.
(Savernake to Castle Cary.)

Station.	Year.	Goods Train Traffic: Forwarded: Coal and Coke "Charged."	Forwarded: Other Minerals.	Forwarded: General Merchandise.	Received: Coal and Coke "Charged."	Received: Other Minerals.	Received: General Merchandise.	Coal and Coke "Not Charged" (Forwarded and Received).	Total Goods Tonnage.	Total Receipts (excluding "Not Charged" Coal and Coke)	Livestock (Forwarded and Received).	Total Carted Tonnage (included in Total Goods Tonnage).
		Tons.	Tons.	Tons.	Tons.	Tons.	Tons.	Tons.	Tons.	£	Wagons.	Tons.
Savernake (Low Level)	1903	—	—	32	14	13	89	59	207	97	3	49
	1913	—	—	140	91	66	327	148	772	433	69	165
	1923	—	—	424	75	461	314	369	1,643	948	12	116
	1924	—	—	112	34	351	360	117	974	638	9	165
	1925	—	—	103	64	447	376	224	1,214	726	6	210
	1926	—	—	74	48	242	307	128	797	552	26	137
	1927	—	23	53	73	1,171	278	128	1,726	992	12	160
	1928	—	—	105	58	652	274	42	1,131	813	44	80
	1929	—	—	80	55	45	224	84	488	528	45	69
	1930	—	—	50	78	33	237	77	475	653	72	66
	1931	—	—	62	90	40	221	82	495	688	99	69
	1932	—	—	20	90	48	165	133	456	606	109	49
	1933	—	4	24	37	80	420	66	631	565	74	58
Burbage Goods. (†)	1903	7	27	1,379	66	68	732	874	3,153	1,204	121	155
	1913	6	22	1,104	74	10	492	996	2,704	1,048	132	163
	1923	—	10	1,284	33	828	452	1,132	3,739	3,722	336	149
	1924	10	20	754	42	1,271	387	1,117	3,601	2,390	256	173
	1925	—	27	790	30	2,030	313	923	4,113	2,057	138	157
	1926	—	326	609	29	1,716	324	318	3,322	2,204	207	128
	1927	—	341	413	59	2,503	425	347	4,088	2,493	202	138
	1928	9	18	376	45	2,852	395	339	4,034	2,295	197	66
	1929	—	129	131	52	2,387	310	234	3,243	2,332	300	47
	1930	—	255	181	50	3,531	329	195	4,541	1,885	128	52
	1931	—	174	234	65	2,469	326	335	3,603	1,663	132	45
	1932	—	19	316	33	1,844	308	389	2,909	1,259	51	88
	1933	—	—	25	37	799	421	433	1,715	651	44	234
Marlborough (‡)	1923	18	184	1,248	163	715	1,355	4,472	8,155	4,352	340	—
	1924	102	111	964	413	3,443	1,157	4,811	11,001	5,020	213	765
	1925	35	121	996	841	3,680	1,044	5,682	12,399	5,114	256	475
	1926	19	109	295	884	3,643	409	4,041	9,400	3,310	437	3
	1927	62	114	64	1,162	3,972	546	5,679	11,599	3,686	350	7
	1928	34	88	182	565	1,507	445	6,065	8,886	2,153	362	13
	1929	—	122	94	892	1,686	401	7,677	10,872	2,579	414	5
	1930	9	228	106	1,111	3,059	564	9,627	14,704	3,104	431	6
	1931	2	266	2,185	1,347	11,837	533	7,934	24,104	6,517	307	25
	1932	8	521	4,098	1,651	1,363	444	7,441	15,526	5,619	279	14
	1933	59	943	2,096	1,611	4,458	4,349	9,597	23,113	10,208	315	3,348
Savernake (High Level) (§)	1923	—	—	199	—	26	231	202	658	727	131	213
	1924	—	—	43	198	174	241	130	786	849	217	24
	1925	—	—	52	161	59	144	318	734	477	157	27
	1926	—	—	33	101	23	158	234	549	527	174	30
	1927	—	—	54	215	40	180	393	882	574	174	37
	1928	—	—	32	203	34	121	513	903	771	222	10
	1929	—	—	70	156	34	102	587	949	566	171	5
	1930	—	—	32	254	42	77	586	991	611	108	7
	1931	—	6	6	282	53	79	513	939	439	80	—
	1932	—	—	4	342	—	68	401	815	361	51	10
	1933	—	—	17	330	6	96	216	665	418	43	26
Grafton & Burbage.	1923	—	63	2,622	33	1,348	1,462	3,116	8,644	5,961	375	258
	1924	—	126	876	67	3,094	1,674	2,244	8,081	3,053	34	110
	1925	—	—	1,368	53	3,864	1,651	2,306	9,262	3,993	23	142
	1926	11	20	1,222	145	4,983	1,651	1,792	9,824	4,135	39	107
	1927	20	150	848	122	3,252	1,651	2,826	8,869	3,330	20	117
	1928	—	12	567	200	1,941	882	2,561	6,163	1,842	38	81
	1929	—	62	639	96	2,019	744	2,532	6,092	1,857	62	47
	1930	—	94	1,085	134	1,566	398	2,203	5,480	2,216	171	43
	1931	—	64	1,025	126	429	263	2,419	4,326	1,377	42	44
	1932	—	—	653	117	391	243	2,294	3,698	1,074	24	29
	1933	5	45	574	94	532	848	1,991	3,589	1,137	17	74